AF541557

Ecological Resources: Conservation and Management

ECOLOGICAL RESOURCES:
CONSERVATION AND MANAGEMENT

Dr. Aluri Jacob Solomon Raju

Prints Publications Pvt Ltd
New Delhi

Published by

Prints Publications Pvt Ltd
Viraj Tower-2, 4259/3, Ansari Road,
Darya Ganj, New Delhi-110002
Tel. : +91-11-45355555
Fax: +91-11-23275542
E-mail : contact@printspublications.com
Website : www.printspublications.com

First Edition : 2022 (Hardbound)

ISBN: 978-93-936742-2-7

Price: ₹ 995/-

Published and Printed by Mr. Pranav Gupta (Director) on behalf of Prints Publications Pvt Ltd, New Delhi.

CONTENTS

PREFACE

The importance of ecological resources is being realized in recent times in view of the global warming and climate change. The ecological resources represent biological resources which in turn have relationship and form other resources such as water, food, etc. This subject is receiving greater attention in recent times due to shortage of food, water and biological resources. Ecological resources are the base for sustaining life in the first place and then sustaining various human lifestyles and civilizations in different parts of the world. This subject is very important for the students, researchers and academicians of botany, zoology, forestry, agriculture, architecture, ecology and evolution, ecotourism, eco-restoration, management, etc.

I have been able to gather material from different sources with great difficulty because the subject itself is in evolving stage, especially in India. This book is a sincere attempt to put together different aspects such as species concept, species inventory, ecosystem functions, impacts and valuation of services, forest resources, biodiversity, biological monitoring, water resources, drought and flood impacts, environmental economics, accounting, costing targets, sustainable architecture, role of information technology in environment, environmental pollution and solid waste management and positive and negative impacts of science and technology. It is an outcome of the compilation and juxtaposition of pertinent information published from different sources including web sources, some of which are anonymous.

I sincerely thank the almighty for giving me the mind, health, time, and life to write the book. I would like to thank my wife, Kamala, my son, Jackson Olive, and daughter, Diamond Celestine, for providing me the necessary moral support. Without their active support, this book would not have seen the light of the day. And I also thank Mr. Pranav Gupta, of Prints Publications Pvt Ltd, New Delhi who readily expressed acceptance and supported me fully for completing this book

Aluri Jacob Solomon Raju

1

ECOSYSTEMS AND ENVIRONMENT

The Concept of Species

A species is one of the basic units of biological classification. It is a fundamental unit of biology as is the cell at a lower level of integration. To elaborate this concept, cells divide to produce new cells, organisms reproduce to generate new organisms and species speciate to produce new species. The rise of a new species from a parental line is called speciation. A species is often defined as a group of organisms capable of interbreeding and producing fertile offspring. It represents a population of individuals which are reproductively isolated from other such groups. In a species, the individuals resemble one another and their genes constantly shuffle around but within their gene pool only. The shared gene pool gives the species its identity; many characteristics can vary within a species. The genes are not transferred to other species.

The species concept is essential to test biological theories and to measure biodiversity. In scientific classification, a species is assigned a two-part name in Latin. The genus is written first with its leading letter capitalized and followed by a species name. Each species is placed within a single genus. There is no clear line demarcating the ancestral species from the descendant species. Although the current scientific understanding of species suggests that there is no rigorous and comprehensive way to distinguish between different species in all cases, biologists continue to seek concrete ways to operationalize the idea. One of the most popular biological definitions of species is in terms of reproductive isolation; if two creatures cannot reproduce to produce fertile offspring, then they are in different species. This definition captures a number of intuitive species boundaries, but it remains imperfect. It has nothing to say about species that reproduce asexually, for example, and it is very difficult to apply to extinct species.

1. Morphological species concept: Species are the smallest natural populations permanently separated from each other by a distinct discontinuity in the series of biotype.

2. Biological species concept: A species is a group of interbreeding natural populations unable to successfully mate or reproduce with other such groups, and which occupies a specific niche in nature.

3. Phylogenetic species concept: A species is the smallest group of organisms that is diagnosably distinct from other such clusters and within which there is a parental pattern of ancestry and descent.

Despite their differences, all species concepts are based on the understanding that there are parameters that make a species a discrete and identifiable evolutionary entity. If populations of a species become isolated, either through differences in their distribution (geographic isolation) or through differences in their reproductive biology (reproductive isolation), they can diverge, ultimately resulting in speciation. During this process, distinct populations representing incipient species - species in the process of formation is expected.

Species Inventory

It is the discovery of all life forms on Earth. It will give us for the first time a complete list of who is here, the roster of fellow inhabitants. It will provide a reliable baseline for counting populations and determining endangered species. It will form the foundation for developing a complete genome of all life and a new understanding of nature. It will uncover multitudes of new species many of which will have immediate cultural and economic impacts. It will train many people as naturalists and scientists who can leverage these skills further in their own lines and that of society. It will distribute wealth from the developed world to far corners of the Earth by employing indigenous and native observers and collectors.

Ecology

Ecology is the scientific study of the distribution and abundance of living organisms and the interactions among organisms and between organisms and their environment. The environment of an organism includes both physical properties, which can be described as the sum of local abiotic factors such as insolation (sunlight), climate, and geology, and biotic factors, which are other living organisms that share its habitat. Organisms can be studied at many different levels, from proteins and nucleic acids (in biochemistry and molecular biology), to cells (in cellular biology), to individuals (in botany, zoology and other similar disciplines) and finally at the level of populations, communities, and ecosystems, to the biosphere as a whole; these latter strata are the primary subjects of ecological inquiry. Ecology is a multi-disciplinary science. Because of its focus on the higher levels of the organization of life on earth and on the interrelations between organisms and their environment, ecology draws heavily on many other branches of science, especially geology and geography, meteorology, pedology, genetics, chemistry and physics. Thus, ecology is considered by some to be a holistic science, one that over-arches older disciplines such as biology which in this view becomes sub-disciplines contributing to ecological knowledge.

The ecosystem is of two entities, the entirety of life, the biocoenosis, and the medium that life exists in, the biotope. Within the ecosystem, species are connected by food chains or food webs. Energy from the sun, captured by primary producers via photosynthesis, flows upward through the chain to primary consumers (herbivores), and then to secondary and tertiary consumers (carnivores and omnivores), before ultimately being lost to the system as waste heat. In the process, matter is incorporated into living organisms, which return their nutrients to the system via decomposition, forming biogeochemical cycles such as the carbon and nitrogen cycles.

Organisms represented in food chain: Primary producers, or autotrophs, are species capable of producing complex organic substances from an energy source and inorganic materials. These organisms are typically photosynthetic plants, bacteria or algae, but in rare cases, like those organisms forming the base of deep-sea vent food webs, can be chemotrophic. Organisms that get their energy by consuming organic substances are called heterotrophs. Heterotrophs include herbivores, which obtain their energy by consuming live plants; carnivores, which obtain energy from consuming live animals; as well as detritivores, scavengers and decomposers, which all consume dead biomass. Energy enters the food chain from the sun. Some energy and/or biomass is lost at each stage of the food chain as faeces (solid waste), movement energy and heat energy (especially by birds and mammals). Therefore, only a small amount of energy and biomass is incorporated into consumer's body and transferred to the next feeding level, thus showing a Pyramid of Biomass.

Energy Flow

A major process linking the abiotic and biotic constituents of ecosystem is the flow of energy. The main source of energy in almost all natural ecosystems is radiant energy from the sun. Primary producers or autotrophic organisms, such as plants, algae, and photosynthetic bacteria, take radiant energy and fix it into organic molecules by photosynthesis, such as creating glucose from carbon dioxide. Only a small portion of radiant energy is actually converted into biochemical form via photosynthesis. Autotrophs are at the base of food chains. Heterotrophs utilize the energy fixed in organic molecules by autotrophs. Herbivores, or primary consumers, are heterotrophs that eat autotrophs, Carnivores are heterotrophs that eat herbivores or other. Carnivores can be secondary consumers (those that eat an herbivore), or tertiary consumers (those that eat a carnivore that has eaten an herbivore), and so on. Omnivores are heterotrophs that consume either autotrophs (primary producers) or consumers (herbivores and carnivores), and include bears and humans. Scavengers, such as crows are heterotrophs that feed on recently dead organisms. Decomposers are heterotrophs that obtain energy by breaking down dead organisms into their inorganic form, such as bracket fungi that break down dead tissues and wastes into carbon, nitrogen, and other inorganic compounds and elements. Autotrophs can then utilize these materials and use them in manufacturing food.

Energy flows through an ecosystem in the form of carbon-carbon bonds. As carbon-carbon bonds are broken, energy is released, which then can be used by the organism or dissipated as heat. Although energy flows through an ecosystem, only a portion of the energy available to an organism is actually stored by the organism, and thus the total energy in one trophic level never flows to the next level. That is, lower trophic levels always contain more total energy than higher trophic levels. Energy does not recycle, but ultimately all energy that is brought into an ecosystem is lost as heat.

System Ecology

System is a set of interacting or interdependent entities, real or abstract, forming an integrated whole. The concept of an 'integrated whole' can also be stated in terms of a system embodying a set of relationships which are differentiated from relationships of the set to other elements, and from relationships between an element of the set and elements not a part of the relational regime.

There are natural and man-made systems. Man-made systems normally have a certain purpose, set of objectives. They are "designed to work as a coherent entity". Natural systems may not have an apparent objective but they are sustainable, efficient and resilient.

A system is a fundamental concept of systems theory, which views the world as a complex system of interconnected parts. We determine a system by choosing the relevant interactions we want to consider, plus choosing the system boundary or, equivalently, providing membership criteria to determine which entities are part of the system, and which entities are outside of the system and are therefore part of the environment of the system. We then make simplified representations (models) of the system in order to understand it and to predict or impact its

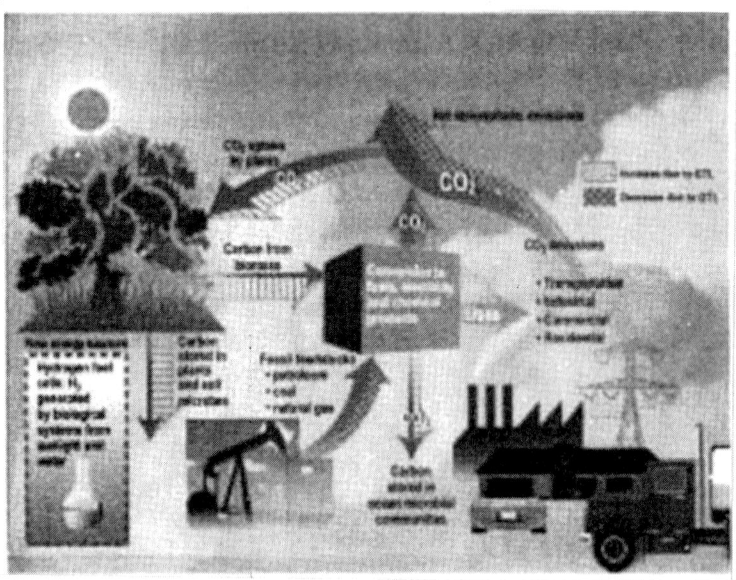

Ecological analysis of CO_2 in ecosystem

future behavior. An open system usually interacts with some entities in their environment. A closed system is isolated from its environment.

System ecology is an interdisciplinary field of ecology, taking a holistic approach to the study of ecological systems, especially ecosystems. System ecology can be seen as an application of general systems theory to ecology. Central to the system ecology approach is the idea that an ecosystem is a complex system exhibiting emergent properties. System ecology focuses on interaction and transaction within and between biological and ecological systems, and is especially concerned with the way the functioning of ecosystems can be influenced by human interventions.

Ecosystem – Functions, Impacts of Changes and Valuation of Services

The term ecosystem was coined in 1930 by Roy Clapham, to denote the physical and biological components of an environment in relation to each other as a unit. British ecologist Arthur Tansley later refined the term, describing it as the interactive system established between biocoenosis (a group of living creatures) and their biotope (the environment in which they live). An ecosystem is a natural unit consisting of all plants, animals and microorganisms in an area functioning together with all the non-living physical factors of the environment. Central to the ecosystem concept is that living organisms are continually engaged in a set of relationships with every other element constituting the environment in which they exist. Ecosystems describe the relationship between organisms and their environment. A system as small as a household or university, or as large as a nation state, may then be suitably discussed as a human ecosystem. While they may be bounded and individually discussed, human ecosystems do not exist independently, but interact in a complex web of human and ecological relationships connecting all human ecosystems to make up the biosphere. As virtually no surface of the earth today is free of human contact, all ecosystems can be more accurately considered as human ecosystems.

Examples of ecosystem are aquatic ecosystem, coral reef ecosystem, desert ecosystem, human ecosystem, marine ecosystem, rainforest ecosystem, savanna ecosystem, taiga ecosystem, tundra ecosystem, urban ecosystem, etc. Within each ecosystem, there are habitats which may also vary in size. A population is a group of living organisms of the same kind living in the same place at the same time. All of the populations interact and form a community. The community of living things interacts with the non-living world around it to form the ecosystem. The habitat must supply the needs of organisms, such as food, water, temperature, oxygen, and minerals. If the population's needs are not met, it will move to a better habitat. Two different populations can not occupy the same niche at the same time, however. It means that the processes of competition, predation, cooperation, and symbiosis occur.

Habitat is the area where a particular species lives. It was originally defined as the physical conditions that surround a species, or species population, or assemblage of species, or community. It is essentially the natural environment in which an organism lives—at least the physical environment—that surrounds or influences and is utilized by a species population. A microhabitat or microenvironment is the immediate surroundings and other physical factors of an individual plant or animal within its habitat. Habitats support different communities of plants and animals. They change constantly due to natural and man-made factors. Natural factors include drought, disease, fire, hurricanes, volcanoes and earthquakes. Man-made factors include urbanization, agriculture, manufac-turing, recreation and transportation. The impact of these two kinds of factors on habitats and their plant and animals need to be understood. In this connection, it is to be noted that carrying capacity of the habitat is important. The carrying capacity of a given habitat means the largest number of individual, a habitat can support for a long period of time. Further, indicator species also tells us about the health of the habitat. Indicator species is a species whose condition provides information on the overall health of the habitat or ecosystem including the health of other species in that ecosystem.

Habitat destruction is a process of land-use change in which one habitat type is removed and replaced with another habitat type. In the process of land-use change, plants and animals which previously used the site are displaced or destroyed, reducing biodiversity. Urban sprawl is one cause of habitat destruction. Other important causes of habitat destruction include mining, trawling, agriculture, industrial activities, etc.

Habitat fragmentation is a process of environmental change important in evolution and conservation biology. As the name implies, it describes the emergence of discontinuities in an organism's preferred habitat. It can be caused by geological processes that slowly alter the layout of the physical environment or by human activity such as land conversion, which can alter the environment on a much faster time scale. The former is suspected to be one of the major causes of speciation while the latter is the causative factor in the extinction of many species. When native vegetation is cleared for human activities such as agriculture, rural development or urbanization, this activity leads to habitat fragmentation. Habitats which were once continuous become divided into separate fragments. After intensive clearing, the separate fragments tend to be very small islands isolated from each other by crop land, pasture, pavement, or even barren land. The latter is often the result of slash and burn farming in tropical forests. Habitat fragmentation may include six discrete processes: reduction in the total area of the habitat, increase in the amount of edge, decrease in the amount of interior habitat, isolation of one habitat fragment from other areas of habitat, breaking up of one patch of habitat into several smaller patches, and decrease in the average size of each patch of habitat.

Ecosystem services are the benefits provided by ecosystems. These include provisioning services such as food, water, timber, fiber, and genetic resources; regulating services such as the regulation of climate, floods, disease, and water quality as well as waste treatment; cultural services such as recreation, aesthetic enjoyment, and spiritual fulfillment; and supporting services such as soil formation, pollination, and nutrient cycling. Human use of all ecosystem services is growing rapidly. Humans have enhanced production of three ecosystem services - crops, livestock and aquaculture - through expansion of the area devoted to their production or through technological inputs. Recently, the service of carbon sequestration has been enhanced globally, due in part to the re-growth of forests in temperate regions, although previously deforestation had been a net source of carbon emissions.

The structure of the world's ecosystems has changed more rapidly in the second half of the twentieth century than at any time in recorded human history, and virtually all of Earth's ecosystems have now been significantly transformed through human actions. The most significant change in the structure of ecosystems has been the transformation of approximately one quarter of Earth's terrestrial surface to cultivated systems. More land was converted to cropland in the 30 years after 1950 than in the 150 years between 1700 and 1850. Between 1960 and 2000, reservoir storage capacity quadrupled; as a result, the amount of water stored behind large dams is estimated to be three to six times the amount held by natural river channels. Although the most rapid changes in ecosystems are now taking place in developing countries, industrial countries have historically experienced comparable rates of change. Croplands expanded rapidly in Europe after 1700 and in North America and the former Soviet Union, particularly after 1850. Roughly, 70% of the original temperate forests and grasslands and Mediterranean forests had been lost by 1950, largely through conversion to agriculture. Historically, deforestation has been much more intensive in temperate regions than in the tropics, and Europe is the continent with the smallest fraction of its original forests remaining. However, changes prior to the industrial era seemed to occur at much slower rates than current transformations.

The ecosystems and biomes that have been most significantly altered globally by human activity include marine and freshwater ecosystems, temperate broadleaf forests, temperate grasslands, mediterranean forests, and tropical dry forests. Within marine systems, the world's demand for food and animal feed over the last 50 years has resulted in fishing pressure so strong that the biomass of both targeted species and those caught incidentally has been reduced in much of the world to one tenth of the levels prior to the onset of industrial fishing. Globally, the degradation of fisheries is also reflected in the fact that the fish being harvested are increasingly coming from the less valuable lower trophic levels as populations of higher trophic level species are depleted. Freshwater ecosystems have been modified through the creation of dams and through the withdrawal of water for human-use. The construction of dams and other structures along rivers has moderately or strongly affected flows in 60% of the large river systems in the world. Water removal for human uses has reduced the flow of several major rivers, to the extent that they do not always flow to the sea. As water flows have declined, so have sediment flows, which are the source of nutrients important for the maintenance of estuaries. Worldwide, sediment delivery to estuaries has declined by roughly 30%. Within terrestrial ecosystems, more than two thirds of the area of two of the world's fourteen major terrestrial biomes (Temperate grasslands and Mediterranean forests) and more than half of the area of four other biomes (tropical dry forests, temperate broadleaf forests, tropical grassland and flooded grasslands) had been converted primarily to agriculture by 1990. Among the major biomes, only tundra and boreal forests show negligible levels of loss and conversion, although they have begun to be affected by climate change.

Globally, the rate of conversion of ecosystems has begun to slow largely due to reductions in the rate of expansion of cultivated land, and in some regions, particularly in temperate zones, ecosystems are returning to conditions and species compositions similar to their pre-conversion states. Yet, rates of ecosystem conversion remain high or are increasing for specific ecosystem and region.

The quantity of provisioning ecosystem services such as food, water, and timber used by humans increased rapidly, often more rapidly than population growth although generally slower than the economic growth, during the second half of the twentieth century. In a number of cases, provisioning services are being used at unsustainable rates. The growing human-use of resources has been made possible by a combination of substantial increases in the absolute amount of some services produced by ecosystems and an increase in the fraction used by humans. World population doubled between 1960 and 2000; from 3 billion to 6 billion people and the global economy increased more than six fold. During this time, food production increased by roughly two-and-a-half times, water-use doubled, wood harvests for pulp and paper tripled, and timber production increased by nearly manifold. The sustainability of the use of provisioning services differs in different locations. However, the use of several provisioning services is unsustainable even in the global aggregate. The current level of use of capture fisheries (marine and freshwater) is not sustainable, and many fisheries have already collapsed. Currently, one quarter of important commercial fish stocks are overexploited or significantly depleted. From 5% to possibly 25% of global freshwater-use exceeds long-term accessible supplies and is maintained only through engineered water transfers or the overdraft of groundwater supplies. Between 15% and 35% of irrigation withdrawals exceed supply rates and are therefore unsustainable. Current agricultural practices are also unsustainable in some regions due to their reliance on unsustainable sources of water, harmful impacts caused by excessive nutrient or pesticide use, salinization, nutrient depletion, and loss that exceeds rates of soil formation.

Humans have substantially altered regulating services such as disease and climate regulation by modifying the ecosystem providing the service and, in the case of waste processing services, by exceeding the capabilities of ecosystems to provide the service. Most changes to regulating services are inadvertent result of actions taken to enhance the supply of provisioning services. Humans have substantially modified the climate regulation service of ecosystems— first through land-use changes that contributed to increases in the amount of carbon dioxide and other greenhouse gases such as methane and nitrous oxide in the atmosphere and more recently by increasing the sequestration of carbon dioxide. Modifications of ecosystems have altered patterns of disease by increasing or decreasing habitat for certain diseases or their vectors or by bringing human populations into closer contact with various disease organisms. Changes to ecosystems have contributed to a significant rise in the number of floods and major wildfires on all continents since the 1940s. Ecosystems serve an important role in detoxifying wastes introduced into the environment, but there are intrinsic limits to that waste processing capability. For example, aquatic ecosystems "cleanse" on average 80% of their global incident nitrogen loading, but this intrinsic self-purification capacity varies widely and is being reduced by the loss of wetlands.

Although the use of cultural services has continued to grow, the capability of ecosystems to provide cultural benefits has been significantly diminished in the past century. Human cultures are strongly influenced by ecosystems, and ecosystem change can have a significant impact on cultural identity and social stability. Human cultures, knowledge systems, religions, heritage values, social interactions, and the linked amenity services such as aesthetic enjoyment, recreation, artistic and spiritual fulfillment, and intellectual development have always been influenced and shaped by the nature of the ecosystem and ecosystem conditions. Many of these benefits are being degraded, either through changes to ecosystems or through societal changes that reduce people's recognition or appreciation of those cultural benefits. Rapid loss of culturally valued ecosystems and landscapes can contribute to social disruptions and societal marginalization. There has been a decline in the quantity and quality of aesthetically pleasing natural landscapes.

Global gains in the supply of food, water, timber, and other provisioning services were often achieved in the past century despite local resource depletion and local restrictions on resource use by shifting production and harvest to new underexploited regions, sometimes considerable distances away. These options are diminishing. This trend is most distinct in the case of marine fisheries. As individual stocks have been depleted, fishing pressure has shifted to less exploited stocks. Industrial fishing fleets have also shifted to fishing further offshore and in deeper water to meet global demand. Although human demand for ecosystem services continues to grow in the aggregate, the demand for particular services in specific regions is declining as substitutes are developed. For example, kerosene, electricity, and other energy sources are increasingly being substituted for fuel wood. The substitution of a variety of other materials for wood such as vinyl, plastics, and metal has contributed to relatively slow growth in global timber consumption in recent years. While the use of substitutes can reduce pressure on specific ecosystem services, this may not always have positive net environmental benefits. Substitution of fuel wood by fossil fuels, for example, reduces pressure on forests and lowers indoor air pollution, but it may increase net greenhouse gas emissions. Substitutes are also often costlier to provide than the original ecosystem services.

Both the supply and the resilience of ecosystem services are affected by changes in biodiversity. When a species is lost from a particular location (even if it does not go extinct globally) or introduced to a new location, the various ecosystem services associated with that species are changed. More generally, when a habitat is converted, an array of ecosystem services associated with the species present in that location is changed, often with direct and immediate impacts on people. Changes in biodiversity also have numerous indirect impacts on ecosystem services over longer time periods, including influencing the capacity of ecosystems to adjust to changing environments, causing disproportionately large and sometimes irreversible changes in ecosystem processes, influencing the potential for infectious disease transmission, and, in agricultural systems, influencing the risk of crop failure in a variable environment and altering the potential impacts of pests and pathogens.

The modification of an ecosystem to alter one ecosystem service, to increase food or timber production, for instance, generally results in changes to other ecosystem services as well. Trade-offs among ecosystem services are commonplace. For example, actions to increase food production often involve one or more aspects such as increased water use, degraded water quality, reduced biodiversity, reduced forest cover, loss of forest products, or release of greenhouse gases. Frequent cultivation, irrigated rice production, livestock production, and burning of cleared areas and crop residues now release 1,600 ± 800 million tonnes of carbon per year in CO_2. Cultivation, irrigated rice production, and livestock production release between 106 and 201 million tonnes of carbon per year in methane. About 70% of anthropogenic nitrous oxide gas emissions are attributed to agriculture, mostly from land conversion and nitrogen fertilizer use. Similarly, the conversion of forest to agriculture can significantly change flood frequency and magnitude, although the amount and direction of this impact is highly dependent on the characteristics of the local ecosystem and the nature of the land cover change. Many trade-offs associated with ecosystem services are expressed in areas remote from the site of degradation. These trade-offs are rarely taken fully into account in decision-making, partly due to the sectoral nature of planning and partly because some of the effects are also displaced in time. The net benefits gained through actions to increase the productivity or harvest of ecosystem services have been less than initially believed after taking into account negative trade-offs. The benefits of resource management actions have traditionally been evaluated only from the standpoint of the service targeted by the management intervention. However, management interventions to increase any particular service almost always result in costs to other services. Negative trade-offs are commonly found between provisioning services and the combined regulating, cultural, and supporting services and biodiversity. Expansion of livestock production around the world has often led to overgrazing and dry land degradation, rangeland fragmentation, loss of wildlife habitat, dust formation, bush encroachment, deforestation, nutrient overload through disposal of manure and greenhouse gas emissions. Agro-forestry can meet human needs for food and fuel, restore soils, and contribute to biodiversity conservation. Intercropping can increase yields, increase bio-control, reduce soil erosion, and reduce weed invasion in fields. Urban parks and other urban green spaces provide spiritual, aesthetic, educational, and recreational benefits as well as such services such as water purification, wildlife habitat, waste management, and carbon sequestration. Protection of natural forests for biodiversity conservation can also reduce carbon emissions and protect water supplies. Protection of wetlands can contribute to flood control and also help to remove pollutants such as phosphorus and nitrogen from water.

Changes in ecosystem services influence all components of human well-being, including the basic material needs for a good life, health, good social relations, security, and freedom of choice and action. Humans are fully dependent on Earth's ecosystems and the services that they provide, such as food, clean water, disease regulation, climate regulation, spiritual fulfillment, and aesthetic enjoyment. The relationship between ecosystem services and human well-being is mediated by access to manufactured, human and social capital. Human well-being depends on ecosystem services but also on the supply and quality of social capital, technology and institutions. These factors mediate the relationship between ecosystem services and human well-being in ways that remain contested and incompletely understood. The relationship between human well-being and ecosystem services is not linear. When an ecosystem service is abundant relative to the demand, a marginal increase in ecosystem services generally contributes only slightly to human well-being. But when the service is relatively scarce, a small decrease can substantially reduce human well-being.

Ecosystem services contribute significantly to global employment and economic activity. The ecosystem service of food production contributes by far the most to economic activity and employment. Both renewable resources such as ecosystem services and non-renewable resources such as mineral deposits, soil nutrients, and fossil fuels are capital assets. Yet, traditional national accounts do not include measures of resource depletion or of the degradation of renewable resources. As a result, a country could cut its forests and deplete its fisheries, and this would show only as a positive gain to Gross Domestic Product despite the loss of the capital asset. Moreover, many ecosystem services are available freely to those who use them (fresh water in aquifers, for instance, or the use of the atmosphere as a sink for pollutants), and again their degradation is not reflected in standard economic measures. When estimates of the economic losses associated with the depletion of natural assets are factored into measurements of the total wealth of nations, they significantly change the balance sheet of those countries with economies especially dependent on natural resources.

The information available to assess the consequences of changes in ecosystem services for human well-being is relatively limited. Many ecosystem services have not been monitored and it is also difficult to estimate the relative influence of changes in ecosystem services in relation to other social, cultural, and economic factors that also affect human well-being. Most resource management decisions are most strongly influenced by ecosystem services entering markets; as a result, the non-marketed benefits are often lost or degraded. Many ecosystem services, such as the purification of water, regulation of floods, or provision of aesthetic benefits, do not pass through markets. The benefits they provide to society, therefore, are largely unrecorded; only a portion of the total benefits provided by an ecosystem make their way into statistics, and many of these are misattributed. Moreover, for ecosystem services that do not pass through markets there is often insufficient incentive for individuals to invest in maintenance. Typically, even if individuals are aware of the services provided by an ecosystem, they are neither compensated for providing these services nor penalized for reducing them. These non-marketed benefits are often high and sometimes more valuable than the marketed benefits. The total economic value associated with managing ecosystems more sustainability is often higher than the value associated with the conversion of the ecosystem through farming, clear-cut logging, or other intensive uses. For example, the value of conversion of an ecosystem in areas of prime agricultural land or in urban regions often exceeds the total economic value of the intact ecosystem. On the contrary, the economic value of water from forested ecosystems near urban populations, for example, now sometimes exceeds the value of timber in those ecosystems. Economic and employment contributions from ecotourism, recreational hunting, and fishing have all grown.

Increased trade has often helped meet growing demand for ecosystem services such as grains, fish, and timber in regions where their supply is limited. While this lessens pressures on ecosystem services within the importing region, it increases pressures in the exporting region. Trade in commodities such as grain, fish, and timber is accompanied by a "virtual trade" in other ecosystem services that are required to support the production of these commodities.

Changes in ecosystem services affect people living in urban ecosystems both directly and indirectly. Likewise, urban populations have strong impacts on ecosystem services both in the local vicinity and at considerable distances from urban centers. Almost half of the world's population now lives in urban areas, and this proportion is growing. Urban development often threatens the availability of water, air and water quality, waste processing, and many other qualities of the ambient environment that contribute to human well-being, and this degradation is particularly threatening to vulnerable groups such as poor people. A wide range of ecosystem services are still important to livelihoods. Urban populations affect distant ecosystems through trade and consumption and are affected by changes in distant ecosystems that affect the local availability or price of commodities, air or water quality, or global climate, or that affect socio-economic conditions in those countries in ways that influence the economy, demographic, or security situation in distant urban areas. The degradation of ecosystem services is harming many of the world's poorest people and is sometimes the principal factor causing poverty. This is not to say that ecosystem changes such as increased food production have not also helped to lift hundreds of millions of people out of poverty. But these changes have harmed many other communities, and their plight has been largely overlooked.

The pattern of "winners" and "'losers" associated with ecosystem changes, and in particular the impact of ecosystem changes on poor people, women, and indigenous peoples, has not been adequately taken into account in management decisions. Changes in ecosystems typically yield benefits for some people and exact costs on others, who may either loose access to resources or livelihoods or be affected by externalities associated with the change. Many changes have been associated with the privatization of what were formerly common pool resources, and the individuals who are dependent on those resources have thus lost rights to them. This has been particularly the case for indigenous peoples, forest-dependent communities, and other groups relatively marginalized from political and economic sources of power. Some of the people and places affected by changes in ecosystems and ecosystem services are highly vulnerable and poorly equipped to cope with the major ecosystem changes that may occur. Highly vulnerable groups include those whose needs for ecosystem services already exceed the supply, such as people lacking adequate clean water supplies and people living in areas with declining per capita agricultural production. Vulnerability has also increased by the growth of populations in ecosystems at the risk of disasters such as floods or drought, often due to inappropriate policies that have encouraged this growth. Populations are growing in low-lying coastal areas and dry land ecosystems in part due to the growth in these vulnerable populations. The number of natural disasters requiring international assistance has quadrupled over the past four decades. Significant differences between the roles and rights of men and women in many societies led to women's increased vulnerability to changes in ecosystem services. Rural women in developing countries are the main producers of staple crops like rice, wheat, and maize. Because, the gendered division of labor within many societies places responsibility for routine care of the household with women, even when women also play important roles in agriculture, the degradation of ecosystem services such as water quality or quantity, fuel wood, agricultural or rangeland productivity often results in increased labor demands on women. This can affect the larger household by diverting time from food preparation, child care, education of children, and other beneficial activities. Yet gender bias persists in agricultural policies in many countries, and rural women involved in agriculture tend to be the last to benefit from or in some cases are negatively affected by development policies and new technologies. The reliance of the rural poor on ecosystem services is rarely measured and thus typically overlooked in national statistics and in poverty assessments, resulting in inappropriate strategies that do not take into account the role of the environment in poverty reduction. Poor people have historically lost access to ecosystem services disproportionately as demand for those services has grown. Coastal habitats are often converted to other uses, frequently for aquaculture ponds or cage culturing of highly valued species. Despite the fact that the area is still used for food production, local residents are often displaced, and the food produced is usually not for local consumption but for export. Diminished human well-being tends to increase immediate dependence on ecosystem services, and the resultant additional pressure can damage the capacity of those ecosystems to deliver services. As human well-being declines, the options available to people that allow them to regulate their use of natural resources at sustainable levels decline as well. This in turn increases pressure on ecosystem services and can create a downward spiral of increasing poverty and further degradation of ecosystem services.

Dry land ecosystems tend to have the lowest levels of human well-being. The small amount of precipitation and its high variability limit the productive potential of dry lands for settled farming and nomadic pastoralism, and many ways of expanding production result in environmental degradation. The combination of high variability in environmental conditions and relatively high levels of poverty leads to situations where human populations can be extremely sensitive to changes in the ecosystem.

Drivers of Change in Ecosystems

Natural or human-induced factors that directly or indirectly cause a change in an ecosystem are referred to as "drivers." A direct driver unequivocally influences ecosystem processes. An indirect driver operates more diffusely, by altering one or more direct drivers. Drivers affect ecosystem services and human well-being at different spatial and temporal scales, which make both their assessment and their management complex. In the aggregate and at a global scale, there are five indirect drivers of changes in ecosystems and their services: population change, change in economic activity, sociopolitical factors, cultural factors, and technological change. Collectively these factors influence the level of production and consumption of ecosystem services and the sustainability of production. Both economic growth and population growth lead to increased consumption of ecosystem services, although the harmful environmental impacts of any particular level of consumption depend on the efficiency of the technologies used in the production of the service. These factors interact in complex ways in different locations to change pressures on ecosystems and uses of ecosystem services. Driving forces are almost always multiple and interactive, so that a one-to-one linkage between particular driving forces and particular changes in ecosystems rarely exists. Even so, changes in any one of these indirect drivers generally result in changes in ecosystems.

Demographic Drivers

Global population doubled in the past 40 years and increased by 2 billion people in the last 25 years. Developing countries have accounted for most recent population growth in the past quarter-century, but there is now an unprecedented diversity of demographic patterns across regions and countries. Some high-income countries such as the United States are still experiencing high rates of population growth, while some developing countries such as China, Thailand, and North and South Korea have very low rates. In the United States, high population growth is due primarily to high levels of immigration. About half the people in the world now live in urban areas. High-income countries typically have populations that are 70–80% urban. Some developing-country regions, such as parts of Asia, are still largely rural, while Latin America, at 75% urban, is indistinguishable from high-income countries in this regard.

Economic Drivers

Global economic activity increased nearly manifold. With rising per capita income, the demand for many ecosystem services grows. At the same time, the consumption structure changes. In the case of food, for example, as income grows the share of additional income spent on food declines, the importance of starchy staples such as rice, wheat, and potatoes declines, diets include more fat, meat and fish, and fruits and vegetables, and the proportionate consumption of industrial goods and services rises. Taxes and subsidies are important indirect drivers of ecosystem change. Fertilizer taxes or taxes on excess nutrients, for example, provide an incentive to increase the efficiency of the use of fertilizer applied to crops and thereby reduce negative externalities. Currently, many subsidies substantially increase rates of resource consumption and increase negative externalities.

Socio-political Drivers

Socio-political drivers encompass the forces influencing decision-making and include the quantity of public participation in decision-making, the groups participating in public decision-making, the mechanisms of dispute resolution, the role of the state relative to the private sector, and levels of education and knowledge. These factors in turn influence the institutional arrangements for ecosystem management, as well as property rights over ecosystem services. There is a declining trend in centralized authoritarian governments and a rise in elected democracies. The role of women is changing in many countries, average levels of formal education are increasing, and there has been a rise in civil society. The trend toward democratic institutions has helped give power to local communities, especially women and resource-poor households. There has been an increase in multilateral environmental agreements. The importance of the state relative to the private sector as a supplier of goods and services, as a source of employment, and as a source of innovation is declining.

Cultural and Religious Drivers

To understand culture as a driver of ecosystem change, it is most useful to think of it as the values, beliefs, and norms that a group of people share. In this sense, culture conditions individuals' perceptions of the world, influence what they consider important, and suggest what courses of action are appropriate and inappropriate. Broad comparisons of whole cultures have not proved useful because they ignore vast variations in values, beliefs, and norms within cultures. Nevertheless, cultural differences clearly have important impacts on direct drivers. Cultural factors, for example, can influence consumption behavior as to what and how much people consume and values related to environmental stewardship, and they may be particularly important drivers of environmental change.

Science and Technology as a Driver

The development and diffusion of scientific knowledge and technologies that exploit that knowledge has profound implications for ecological systems and human well-being. The twentieth century saw tremendous advances in understanding how the world works physically, chemically, biologically, and socially and in the applications of that knowledge to human endeavors. The impact of science and technology on ecosystem services is most evident in the case of food production. Much of the increase in agricultural output over the past four decades has come from an increase in yields per hectare rather than an expansion of area under cultivation. At the same time, technological advances can also lead to the degradation of ecosystem services. Advances in fishing technologies, for example, have contributed significantly to the depletion of marine fish stocks.

Consumption of ecosystem services is slowly being decoupled from economic growth. Growth in the use of ecosystem services over the past five decades was generally much less than the growth in GDP. This change reflects structural changes in economies, but it also results from new technologies and new management practices and policies that have increased the efficiency with which ecosystem services are used and provided substitutes for some services. Even with this progress, though, the absolute level of consumption of ecosystem services continues to grow, which is consistent with the pattern for the consumption of energy and materials.

Global trade magnifies the effect of governance, regulations, and management practices on ecosystems and their services, enhancing good practices but worsening the damage caused by poor practices. Increased trade can accelerate degradation of ecosystem services in exporting countries if their policy, regulatory, and management systems are inadequate. At the same time, international trade enables comparative advantages to be exploited and accelerates the diffusion of more-efficient technologies and practices. The increased demand for forest products in many countries stimulated by growth in forest products trade can lead to more rapid degradation of forests in countries with poor systems of regulation and management, but can also stimulate a "virtuous cycle" if the regulatory framework is sufficiently robust to prevent resource degradation while trade, and profits, increase. While historically most trade related to ecosystems has involved provisioning services such as food, timber, fiber, genetic resources, and biochemicals, one regulating service climate regulation, or more specifically carbon sequestration is now also traded internationally.

Urban demographic and economic growth has been increasing pressures on ecosystems globally, but affluent rural and suburban living often places even more pressure on ecosystems. Dense urban settlement is considered to be less environmentally burdensome than urban and suburban sprawl. And the movement of people into urban areas has significantly lessened pressure on some ecosystems and it has also led to the reforestation of some parts of industrial countries that had been deforested in previous centuries. At the same time, urban centers facilitate human access to and management of ecosystem services.

Coastal ecosystems are affected by multiple direct drivers. Fishing pressures in coastal ecosystems are compounded by a wide array of other drivers, including land-, river-, and ocean-based pollution, habitat loss, invasive species, and nutrient loading. The greatest threat to coastal systems is the development-related conversion of coastal habitats such as forests, wetlands, and coral reefs through coastal urban sprawl, resort and port development, aquaculture, and industrialization. Dredging, reclamation and destructive fishing also account for widespread, effectively irreversible destruction. Shore protection structures and engineering works by changing coastal dynamics, have impacts extending beyond their direct footprints. Nitrogen loading to the coastal zone has increased by about 80% worldwide and has driven coral reef community shifts. Over the past four decades, excessive nutrient loading has emerged as one of the most important direct drivers of ecosystem change in terrestrial, freshwater, and marine ecosystems. While the introduction of nutrients into ecosystems can have both beneficial effects such as increased crop productivity and adverse effects such as eutrophication of inland and coastal waters, the beneficial effects will eventually reach a plateau as more nutrients are added while the harmful effects will continue to grow. Synthetic production of nitrogen fertilizer has been an important driver for the remarkable increase in food production that has occurred during the past 50 years. Since excessive nutrient loading is largely the result of applying more nutrients than crops can use, it harms both farm incomes and the environment. Excessive flows of nitrogen contribute to eutrophication of freshwater and coastal marine ecosystems and acidification of freshwater and terrestrial ecosystems with implications for biodiversity in these ecosystems. To some degree, nitrogen also plays a role in the creation of ground-level ozone which leads to loss of agricultural and forest productivity, destruction of ozone in the stratosphere which leads to depletion of the ozone layer and increased UV-B radiation on Earth, causing increased incidence of skin cancer, and climate change.

The resulting health effects include the consequences of ozone pollution on asthma and respiratory function, increased allergies and asthma due to increased pollen production, the risk of blue-baby syndrome, increased risk of cancer and other chronic diseases from nitrates in drinking water, and increased risk of a variety of pulmonary and cardiac diseases from production of fine particles in the atmosphere. Phosphorus application has increased threefold since 1960, with a steady increase until 1990 followed by a leveling off at a level approximately equal to applications in the 1980s. While phosphorus use has increasingly concentrated on phosphorus-deficient soils, the growing phosphorus accumulation in soils contributes to high levels of phosphorus runoff. As with nitrogen loading, the potential consequences include eutrophication of coastal and freshwater ecosystems, which can lead to degraded habitat for fish and decreased quality of water for consumption by humans and livestock. Many ecosystem services are reduced when inland water and coastal ecosystems become eutrophic. Water from lakes that experience algal blooms is more expensive to purify for drinking or other industrial uses. Eutrophication can reduce or eliminate fish populations. Possibly the most apparent loss in services is the loss of many of the cultural services provided by lakes. Foul odors of rotting algae, slime-covered lakes, and toxic chemicals produced by some blue-green algae during blooms keep people from swimming, boating, and otherwise enjoying the aesthetic value of lakes.

Climate change in the past century has already had a measurable impact on ecosystems. Earth's climate system has changed since the pre-industrial era, in part due to human activities, and it is projected to continue to change throughout the twenty-first century. During the last 100 years, the global mean surface temperature has increased by about 0.6°C, precipitation patterns have changed spatially and temporally, and global average sea level rose by 0.1-0.2 meters. Observed changes in climate, especially warmer regional temperatures, have already affected biological systems in many parts of the world. There have been changes in species distributions, population sizes, and the timing of reproduction or migration events, as well as an increase in the frequency of pest and disease outbreaks, especially in forested systems.

Valuation of Ecosystem Services

The simplest form of ecosystem valuation is to hold that an ecosystem has a value equivalent to its ecological yield valued as it would be on commodity markets: for the value of water, wood, fish or game, that is purified or nurseried or generated or harboured in that ecosystem. Thus, a price can be put on the natural capital of an ecosystem based on the price of natural resources it yields each year. Four types of values can be assigned to ecosystems:

1. Direct-use value - It is the value attributed to direct utilisation of ecosystem services. A living thing's utilitarian value is determined by its use or function. It is measured in terms of its use for humans, such as for medicine or food. However, it can also represent the value of an organism to other living things or its ecological value.

2. Indirect-use value - It is the value attributed to indirect utilisation of ecosystem services, through the positive externalities that ecosystems provide. It describes the inherent worth of an organism, independent of its value to anyone or anything else. All species have intrinsic value and that humans are no more important than other species. Thus everything has an equal right to exist simply because it already exists. Having this right will result in also having a "right" to have ones future survival guaranteed to an extent equal to any or all other

species. If one accepts the idea that biodiversity has intrinsic value, then species conservation requires less justification. In other words, if a species is intrinsically valuable, regardless of its use to humans or to other species, it should be conserved. Intrinsic value is a central tenet of many religions. Many religions consider everything on earth to be inherently sacred, or sacred as a result of being created by a divine being, and thus, intrinsically valuable, and humans are responsible to care for and respect these creations.

3. Option value - It is the value attributed to preserving the option to utilise ecosystem services in the future. It refers to the use that something may have in the future; sometimes this is included as a use value.

4. Non-use value - It is the value attributed to the pure existence of an ecosystem and consists of three components: value-based on the welfare the ecosystem may give to other people; value based on the welfare the ecosystem may give to future generations; and value based on knowing that the ecosystem exists. There are several less tangible values that are sometimes called non-use or passive values, for things that we don't use but would consider as a loss if they were to disappear; these include existence value, the value of knowing something exists even if you will never use it or see it, and the value of knowing something will be there for future generations.

Methods to estimate the value of ecosystem services which cannot be derived from market prices include "stated preference" methods and "revealed preference" methods. Stated preference methods, such as the contingent valuation method - ask people for their willingness to pay for a certain ecosystem service. Revealed preference methods, such as hedonic pricing and the travel cost method, use a relation with a market good or service to estimate the willingness to pay for the service.

Considering "valuation" as an "economic not ecological issue" reflects the way these fields divide of the activities of humans versus non-humans in "making a living". When humans go out to get food or homes, that is studied in "economics", but when non-humans do it, that is "ecology", though it is clear that there are motivations, methods and certainly bodily needs in common. Since animals do not put explicit prices on ecosystems they use, but do behave as if they are valuable, e.g. by defending turf or access to water, it is mostly a matter of definition whether ecology should include valuation as an issue. It may be anthropocentric to do so, since "valuation" more clearly refers to a human perception rather than being an "objective" attribute of the system perceived. Ecology itself is also human perception, and such related concepts as a food chain are constructed by humans to help them understand ecosystems. Determining the value or worth of biodiversity is complex. Economists typically subdivide utilitarian or use values of biodiversity into direct-use value for those goods that are consumed directly, such as food or timber, and indirect-use value for those services that support the items that are consumed, including ecosystem functions like nutrient cycling.

2

LAND AND FORESTS

Land comprises of a bundle of earth materials and vegetation cover. Man has used, overused and abused the land materials in such a way that the land-use pattern is detrimental in the long run for the present and future generations. Changes in land cover occur in two forms: a) Conversion, a process that refers to the change of the cover from one class to another such as when forest is cleared for cropland or when cropland is converted into urban settlement or when wetland drainage is used for cultivation of crops and b) Modification, a process that refers to an alteration of the existing cover that does not convert it to a different type of cover. World over, cultivation has replaced less productive land-uses such as forest wastelands of different kinds. From the dawn of civilization till the present day, land surface has been greatly altered by humankind. Much modern change in the most densely populated lands occurs from one human shaped state to another. Today, much urban construction is actually redevelopment, it is more so in the developed world. Forest that is removed now is not being cut for the first time. The intensification of land-use repeatedly has taken the shape of a worldwide drive for an increase in production keeping pace with the exploding population, growing markets and competition from several producers. At present, an increasing population and ever-increasing human needs and desires have put lots of pressure on forests and resulted in massive deforestation. When forest land is converted into other land-uses particularly urban and industrial, it leaves a serious impact of the environment that is harmful to human society in particular and to life in general on the plant earth.

Human Population Growth

Human population shows an exponential growth. As the population base grows the number of people on earth soars. The distribution of human population is not even over the globe. Several factors are responsible for uneven distribution of human population. The factors that determine the pattern of population distribution are complex and diverse. They include physical and non-physical. The physical factors are geographical location, topography, climate, soil, natural vegetation, rivers, lakes or other water bodies and mineral resources. The non-physical factors include economic development and level of technology, birth and death rates migration and political reasons. Man has the tendency to settle down in areas where he receives the maximum benefits. In doing so, the numbers are either too great or too low for the full utilization of the available resources in certain areas. Human population largely concentrated along the margins of continents. The interiors of continents are sparsely populated. The continental margins provide climatic congeniality and commercial opportunities and hence, human populations concentrate more along the coasts. In India, there is a rapid rate of increase in human population due to high birth rate, low death rate, high rate of immigration from the neighbouring countries and scientific and technological developments and rise in economic standards. Further, food resources are available in surplus amount and hence, our people have opted the principle of feed and breed for increasing human populations.

Human Population Pressure on Land

Human societies have converted or modified the land cover in a variety of ways. Land conversion has resulted in social disruption and reduced vegetation cover. As urban areas expand they swallow up rural land especially flat or rolling land with well drained fertile soil. Each year a greater area of rural and mostly cropland is converted to urban development, highways, industrial areas, residential colleges, etc. Once prime cropland is converted for other purposes, it is lost for food production. As land values near urban areas rise, taxes on nearby cropland increase so much that many farmers are forced to sell their land. They make much more money selling to developers than raising crops. The outward expansion of cities creates numerous problems for nearby rural areas. Narrow country roads and small town streets become congested with the traffic. Town and village health, school, police, fire, water, sanitation and other services are overwhelmed. Air and water pollution, crime, noise and congestion increase. With increasing population growth day by day in developing countries like India, the pressure on land has increased manifold. In some cities due to huge pressure on land, high rise apartments have come into existence and these have further increased pollution problems causing severe health problems to the city dwellers.

Human Population Pressure on Forests

Forest is an important ecosystem. It provides a habitat to different types of plants, animals and micro-organisms. Forests give us nutrient rich soil having high organic matter content. They play a vital role in increasing precipitation, preventing soil erosion, reducing surface *run off*, the frequency and dimension of floods, encouraging percolation of rain water, increasing recharge of ground-water potentials, providing domestic fuel wood to numerous people, providing raw materials to various forest based industries and also offering food and shelter to innumerable animals. The task of assessing the direct and indirect importance of forest land-use is an extremely difficult one. Nevertheless, the forests play a crucial role in the stability of environment and ecosystem and in the restoration of ecological balance.

At present, an increasing human population and an ever-increasing human needs and desires have caused massive deforestation. When forest land is converted into other land-uses particularly urban and industrial it leaves a serious impact on the environment that proves harmful to the society. The most common causes or pressures on forests that resulted in deforestation are conversion of forest covered land into agricultural land, practice of shifting cultivation in hilly terrains, conversion of forest land into pasture lands, over-grazing by animals, lumbering for domestic and commercial interests, natural and man induced forest fires, development of large scale multi-purpose river valley projects, unscrupulous destruction by ambitious timber traders, illiteracy and lack of consciousness among the rural masses, etc. The consequences of deforestation far outweigh the benefits of deforestation. Some such consequences accelerate rate of soil erosion, increase in the sediment load of rivers, siltation of reservoirs and rivers beds, rise in the frequency and dimension of both floods and droughts, changes in the pattern of distribution of precipitation, intensification of green house effect and rise in temperature, intensification of devastating force of atmospheric storms, floods and droughts causing damage to agricultural crops, erosion of fertile top soil that hampers agricultural production, unscrupulous and random felling of trees that affect the supply of raw materials to the industries and building materials to the urban and rural areas, fodder shortage to animals poverty that amplifies the rate of crimes and other social problems, etc.

Forest lands have been replaced by settlement, industry, transportation and communication routes, reservoirs, etc. among which human settlement is the most significant. Today, the pressure on forests is too high. Ecotourism is a new factor that is affecting the forest cover. In the name of ecotourism, the forest cover has been cleared for making roads, construction of hotels, restaurants, etc. With rapid human population growth coupled with diversified needs and desires, forests have been decimated to a great extent. The remaining forest cover is fragile in character because of continued human interference with it for procuring forest based items. If this pressure on forest cover goes unabated soon the forest cover will disappear. A classical example is already there showing the consequences of overuse and abuse of forest cover. There is a small island by name Easter Island which is isolated in the great expanse of the South Pacific. This island was first colonized about 2,500 years ago by Polynesians who brought with them animals and food plants. The civilization they developed was based on the island trees which were used for shelter, tools, boats, fuel food and clothing. Using these resources, they developed an impressive civilization and a technology capable of making large stone structures, including their famous statues. The people flourished and their population reached to a peak of about 10,000. They continued to use the precious trees without any consideration of their renewal. Each person who cuts a tree reaped immediate personal benefits while also helping to doom the civilization as a whole. As they started to run out of the wood that supported them, the people turned to warfare and cannibalism. Both the population and the civilization collapsed soon. In 1772, on the day of Easter (Resurrection day of Jesus Christ), Dutch explorers reached the island and found only about 2,000 inhabitants struggling under primitive conditions on a mostly barren island. Like Easter Island at its peak, the planet Earth is in its own way an isolated island with thriving technological civilization. And like Easter Island, our population is growing and we are consuming exhaustible and potentially renewable resources especially the forest resources at a rapid pace. The question now is, will the humans on Earth Island recreate the tragedy of Easter Island on a grander scale?

Solutions for Pressure Reduction on Land and Forests

As described above the example of Eastern Island is a tragedy of commons which refers to the tendency of individuals to take advantage of a shared resource until it is ruined. In this example, the tragedy resulted in the loss of valuable species of trees, the destruction of a culture and the nearly total loss of the island's human population. In the same manner, consider the Earth as a big island and its common resources are utilized by different populations or societies without considering their sustainability, one day we all will end up with the same tragedy. To stop this situation, we must invent a profitable way to stop using the common resources or reach a collective agreement to take collective action to regulate the use of shared earth's resources. Another important solution is high literacy rates and education levels, especially for women once they are empowered intellectually and socially they make decisions about the number of children they wish to have. Low infant mortality levels give parents a high level of confidence that even with a small family some of their children will grow to maturity carry the family name and genes and provide physical security for their parents when they are old. Political will is required to implement any birth control programme. Simply flooding with condoms, pills and sterilization operations without a number of other simultaneous changes such as literacy, education, health care, etc. will not give expected results to control birth rate. Further, we should also think beyond family planning and offer economic rewards and penalties to help slow population growth. Some countries like China penalize couples who have more than one or two children by raising their taxes, charging other fees, disallowing health care benefits, food allotments and job options. Such coercive methods are unavoidable in any country that is out of control in population growth in order to prevent mass starvation hardship and also reduce pressure on land resources. Judicious use of forest resources will enable us to have these resources sustainable. People who use forest resources must be educated to minimize environmental damage to the forest cover. Each individual should work to curb deforestation, protect the biodiversity and other ecological services provided by the plants, forests and help reforest degraded areas. Chipko movement is the best example to follow. We can still save the remaining forests and the species they harbour. If we fail to do so, there will be nothing left for our successors to do but pick up all the pieces. It is in our hands whether to protect or to swallow land resources especially the forests; which path you choose? We must be wise citizens of this earth and we should not give any scope for the recurrence of the tragedy of Easter Island.

3

FOREST RESOURCES

Historically, "forest" means an uncultivated area which is legally set aside for hunting by feudal nobility and these hunting forests were not necessarily wooded much if at all. There are different definitions for the word "forest". The most significant differences concern the legal classifications of land-uses in a country (forest/agriculture/urban) and the kind of vegetation that constitutes a forest.

Some legal definitions of 'forest' are based on the actual vegetation on the ground, whereas other definitions are based on a defined land area which may have no vegetation on it at all but is legally under the jurisdiction of the national agency which manages forests and natural resources. India's Forest Conservation Act of 1980 states that any land recorded as forest in any land record is legally forest land whether or not there is any vegetation on the land. Forests can be found in all regions capable of sustaining tree growth, at altitudes up to the tree line, except where natural fire frequency is too high, or where the environment has been impaired by natural processes or by human activities. As a general rule, forests dominated by angiosperms (broad-leaf forests) are more species-rich than those dominated by gymnosperms (conifer, montane or needle-leaf forests), although exceptions exist.

Forests sometimes contain many tree species within a small area (as in tropical rain and temperate deciduous forests), or relatively few species over large areas (taiga and arid montane coniferous forests). Forests are often home to many animal and plant species, and biomass per unit area is high compared to other vegetation communities. Much of this biomass occurs below-ground in the root systems and as partially decomposed plant detritus. The woody component of a forest contains lignin, which is relatively slow to decompose compared with other organic materials such as cellulose or carbohydrate.

Types of Forests

Forests can be classified in different ways and to different degrees of specificity. One such way is in terms of the "biome" in which they exist, combined with leaf longevity of the dominant species (whether they are evergreen or deciduous). Another distinction is whether the forests composed predominantly of broad-leaf trees, coniferous (needle-leaved) trees, or mixed.

Boreal forests occupy the subarctic zone and are generally evergreen and coniferous. Temperate zones support both broad-leaf deciduous forests (temperate deciduous forest) and evergreen coniferous forests (temperate coniferous forests and temperate rainforests). Warm temperate zones support broad-leaf evergreen forests, including laurel forests. Tropical and subtropical forests include tropical and subtropical moist forests, tropical and subtropical dry forests, and tropical and subtropical coniferous forests.

Physiognomy classifies forests based on their overall physical structure or developmental stage (old growth vs. second growth). Forests can also be classified more specifically based on the climate and the dominant tree species present, resulting in numerous different forest types. A number of global forest classification systems have been proposed but none has gained universal acceptance. UNEP classification system divides the world's forests into 26 major types, which reflect climatic zones as well as the principal types of trees. These 26 major types can be reclassified into 6 broader categories:

1. **Temperate needle-leaf forests**: Temperate needle-leaf forests mostly occupy the higher latitude regions of the northern hemisphere, as well as high altitude zones and some warm temperate areas, especially on nutrient-poor or otherwise unfavourable soils. These forests are composed entirely, or nearly so, of coniferous species (Coniferophyta). In the Northern Hemisphere *Pinus, Picea, Larix, Abies, Pseudotsuga* and *Tsuga* make up the canopy, but other taxa are also important. In the southern hemisphere most coniferous trees, members of the Araucariaceae and Podocarpaceae, occur in mixtures with broad-leaf species that are classed as broad-leaf and mixed forests.

2. **Temperate broad-leaf and mixed forests**: Temperate broad-leaf and mixed forests include a substantial component of trees in the Anthophyta. They are generally characteristic of the warmer temperate latitudes, but extend to cool temperate ones, particularly in the southern hemisphere. They include such forest types as the mixed deciduous forests of the USA and their counterparts in China and Japan, the broad-leaf evergreen rain forests of Japan, Chile and Tasmania, the sclerophyllous forests of Australia, the Mediterranean and California, and the southern beech Nothofagus forests of Chile and New Zealand.

3. **Tropical moist forests**: Tropical moist forests include many different forest types. The best known and most extensive are the lowland evergreen broad-leaf rainforests. The forests of tropical mountains are also included in this broad category, generally divided into upper and lower montane formations on the basis of their physiognomy, which varies with altitude. The montane forests include cloud forest, those forests at middle to high altitude, which derive a significant part of their water budget from cloud, and support a rich abundance of vascular and non-vascular epiphytes. Mangrove forests also fall within this broad category, as do most of the tropical coniferous forests of Central America.

4. **Tropical dry forests:** Tropical dry forests are characteristic of areas in the tropics affected by seasonal drought. The seasonality of rainfall is usually reflected in the deciduousness of the forest canopy, with most trees being leafless for several months of the year. However, under some conditions, e.g. less fertile soils or less predictable drought regimes, the proportion of evergreen species increases and the forests are characterised as "sclerophyllous". Thorn forest, a dense forest of low stature with a high frequency of thorny or spiny species, is found where drought is prolonged, and especially where grazing animals are plentiful. On very poor soils, and especially where fire is a recurrent phenomenon, woody savannas develop.

5. **Sparse trees and parkland forests**: Sparse trees and parkland are forests with open canopies of 10-30% crown cover. They occur principally in areas of transition from forested to non-forested landscapes. The two major zones in which these ecosystems occur are in the boreal region and in the seasonally dry tropics. At high latitudes, north of the main zone of boreal forest or taiga, growing conditions are not adequate to maintain a continuous closed forest cover, so tree cover is both sparse and discontinuous. This vegetation is variously called open taiga, open lichen woodland, and forest tundra. It is species-poor, has high bryophyte cover, and is frequently affected by fire.

6. **Forest plantations**: Forest plantations, generally intended for the production of timber and pulpwood increase the total area of forest worldwide. Commonly mono-specific and/or composed of introduced tree species, these ecosystems are not generally important as habitat for native biodiversity. However, they can be managed in ways that enhance their biodiversity protection functions and they are important providers of ecosystem services such as maintaining nutrient capital, protecting watersheds and soil structure as well as storing carbon. They may also play an important role in alleviating pressure on natural forests for timber and fuelwood production.

Twenty-six forest categories are used to enable the translation of forest types from national and regional classification systems to a harmonised global one:

Temperate and boreal forest types

1. Evergreen needle-leaf forest: Natural forest with > 30% canopy cover, in which the canopy is predominantly (> 75%) needle-leaf and evergreen.

2. Deciduous needle-leaf forest: Natural forests with > 30% canopy cover, in which the canopy is predominantly (> 75%) needle-leaf and deciduous.

3. Mixed broad-leaf/needle-leaf forest: Natural forest with > 30% canopy cover, in which the canopy is composed of a more or less even mixture of needle-leaf and broad-leaf crowns.

4. Broad-leaf evergreen forest: Natural forests with > 30% canopy cover, the canopy being > 75% evergreen and broad-leaf.

5. Deciduous broad-leaf forest: Natural forests with > 30% canopy cover, in which > 75% of the canopy is deciduous and broad-leaves predominate (> 75% of canopy cover).

6. Freshwater swamp forest: Natural forests with > 30% canopy cover, composed of trees with any mixture of leaf type and seasonality, but in which the predominant environmental characteristic is a waterlogged soil.

7. Sclerophyllous dry forest: Natural forest with > 30% canopy cover, in which the canopy is mainly composed of sclerophyllous broad-leaves and is > 75% evergreen.

8. Disturbed natural forest: Any forest type above that has in its interior significant areas of disturbance by people, including clearing, felling for wood extraction, anthropogenic fires, road construction, etc.

9. Sparse trees and parkland: Natural forests in which the tree canopy cover is between 10-30%, such as in the steppe

regions of the world. Trees of any type - needle-leaf, broad-leaf, palms.

10. Exotic species plantation: Intensively managed forests with > 30% canopy cover, which have been planted by people with species not naturally occurring in that country.

11. Native species plantation: Intensively managed forests with > 30% canopy cover, which have been planted by people with species that occur naturally in that country.

Tropical forest types

12. Lowland evergreen broad-leaf rain forest: Natural forests with > 30% canopy cover, below 1200 m altitude that display little or no seasonality, the canopy being >75% evergreen broad-leaf.

13. Lower montane forest: Natural forests with > 30% canopy cover, between 1200-1800 m altitude, with any seasonality regime and leaf type mixture.

14. Upper montane forest: Natural forests with > 30% canopy cover, above 1800 m altitude, with any seasonality regime and leaf type mixture.

15. Freshwater swamp forest: Natural forests with > 30% canopy cover, below 1200 m altitude, composed of trees with any mixture of leaf type and seasonality, but in which the predominant environmental characteristic is a waterlogged soil.

16. Semi-evergreen moist broad-leaf forest: Natural forests with > 30% canopy cover, below 1200 m altitude in which between 50-75% of the canopy is evergreen, > 75% are broad-leaves, and the trees display seasonality of flowering and fruiting.

17. Mixed broad-leaf/needle-leaf forest: Natural forests with > 30% canopy cover, below 1200 m altitude, in which the canopy is composed of a more or less even mixture of needle-leaf and broad-leaf crowns.

18. Need-leleaf forest: Natural forest with > 30% canopy cover, below 1200 m altitude, in which the canopy is predominantly (> 75%) needle-leaf.

19. Mangroves: Natural forests with > 30% canopy cover, composed of species of mangrove tree, generally along coasts in or near brackish or salt water.

20. Freshwater wetlands: Natural forests with > 10% canopy cover, composed of shrubs and herbs in and around freshwater lakes.

21. Disturbed natural forest: Any forest type above that has in its interior significant areas of disturbance by people, including clearing, felling for wood extraction, anthropogenic fires, road construction, etc.

22. Deciduous/semi-deciduous broad-leaf forest: Natural forests with > 30% canopy cover, below 1200 m altitude in which between 50-100% of the canopy is deciduous and broad-leaves predominate (> 75% of canopy cover).

23. Sclerophyllous dry forest: Natural forests with > 30% canopy cover, below 1200 m altitude, in which the canopy is mainly composed of sclerophyllous broad-leaves and is > 75% evergreen.

24. Thorn forest: Natural forests with > 30% canopy cover, below 1200 m altitude, in which the canopy is mainly composed of deciduous trees with thorns and succulent phanerophytes with thorns, may be frequent.

25. Exotic species plantation - Intensively managed forests with > 30% canopy cover, which have been planted by people with species not naturally occurring in that country.

26. Native species plantation - Intensively managed forests with > 30% canopy cover, which have been planted by people with species that occur naturally in that country.

Uses of Forests

People began life on this planet as forest dwellers. They were food gatherers and depended on the forest for all their needs: food, clothing and shelter. They gradually became food growers, clearing a small patch in the forest to grow food. But they continued to depend on forests to meet a lot of their needs. Even today people depend on the forest for paper, timber, fuel wood, medicine and fodder.

For the rural population, wood is an important source of energy for cooking and heating. They prefer smaller stems as these are easier to collect and carry. The wood that they select should be easy to split and have low moisture content to dry faster. Some of the wood is converted to charcoal and used for cooking. More than 1500 species of trees are commercially exploited for timber in different parts of India. It is used in timber-based industries such as plywood, saw milling, paper and pulp, and particle boards. These are common in the north-eastern and the south-western parts of India, growing along with deciduous or evergreen forest. The main commercial uses of bamboo are as timber substitutes, fodder, and raw material for basket, paper and pulp, and other small-scale industries. Cane or rattan are the stems of a climber plant and are used for a large number of household items. It is used to make walking sticks, polo sticks, baskets, picture frames, screens and mats. Fodder from the forest forms an important source for cattle and other grazing animals in the hilly and the arid regions and during a drought. There are many varieties of grasses, trees, and shrubs that are nutritious for the livestock. Care is taken to see that trees poisonous to cattle are not grown. Trees that produce a large crown above the reach of cattle are preferred. Fences created with trees and shrubs are preferred in developing countries as they are cheap to maintain yet give protection. Species that have thorns or are prickly and have stiff branches and leaves that are not edible are preferred. These species should be fast growing, hardy, and long lived. Trees grown for wind breaks should be bushy and sturdy to withstand strong winds, both hot and cold. Along the Saurashtra coast in India, *Casuarina* has successfully been planted to check degradation due to salt laden coastal winds. *Prosopis juliflora,* planted along the desert border in Haryana and Gujarat has successfully halted the advance of the desert. Tree roots bind the soil and prevent erosion caused by wind or water. Leaf fall also provides a soil cover that further protects the soil. *Casuarina* planted along the coastal region has helped in binding the sand and stabilizing the sand dunes in the area. Some species of trees have the ability to return nitrogen to the soil through root decomposition or fallen leaves. Such trees are planted to increase the nitrogen content of the soil.

Fruit trees are an important source of income and food for the rural household. In some areas fruit trees are commonly planted along the field borders and around the wells. Mango, coconut, orange, pear, jackfruit and many others grow wild in the forest. Since time immemorial humans have been depending on the forest to cure them of various ailments. Even today man is dependent on the forest for herbs and plants to fight against disease. Of all the medicinal trees found in India, the neem is the most important. Leaves, bark, and other part of many other trees also have medicinal value and are used to make various ayurvedic medicines. Tropical grasses such as lemon-grass, citronella, and khus are the source of essential oils. Oil is distilled from the wood of various species such as sandalwood, agar and pine. Oil is also derived from the leaves of certain plants and trees such as eucalyptus, camphor, wintergreen and pine. These oils are used for making soaps, cosmetics, incense, pharmaceuticals, and confectionery. Plant fibre has many different uses. Soft fibres such as jute are derived from the stems of the plant. Hard fibre from the leaves of hemp and sisal are used to make fabrics for various applications. Coir, another form of fibre from the fruit of the coconut, is used to make ropes. The fruits of many species of Indian trees produce silky floss. It is used to make cotton wool, mattresses and pillows.

Biodiversity – Conservation and Management

Biodiversity is the result of 4 billion years of evolution. It is not distributed evenly on Earth. The diversity in any region depends on climate, altitude, soils and the presence of other species. Most of the terrestrial diversity is found in tropical forests. Biodiversity is a term intended to describe all of nature's variety. It refers to the variety of species on the planet; the amount of genetic variation that exists within a species; the diversity of communities in an ecosystem; and the rich variety of landscapes that occur on the planet. In one line, it is the variation of life at all levels of biological organization. In other words, it is the totality of genes, species and ecosystems of a region. Biodiversity hotspots are excellent examples of species diversity. A biodiversity hotspot is a region with a high level of endemic species. Hotspots unfortunately tend to occur near areas of dense human habitation, leading to threats to their many endemic species. As a result of the pressures of the rapidly growing human population, human activity in many of these areas is increasing dramatically. Most of these hotspots are located in the tropics and most of them are forests.

Biodiversity Action Plan (BAP)

On May 22, 1992 the nations of the world adopted the CBD in Nairobi and on June 5, 1992 the CBD was tabled at the UN Conference on Environment and Development in Rio de Janeiro. The Convention on Biological Diversity (CBD) was negotiated and signed by nations at the UNCED Earth Summit at Rio de Janeiro in Brazil in June 1992. The Convention came into force on December 29, 1993. India became a Party to the Convention in 1994. At present, there are 175 Parties to this Convention.

The main objectives of the Convention are:

1. Conservation of biological diversity.
2. Sustainable use of the components of biodiversity.
3. Management structure of Biodiversity Act.

The CBD is the most important international legal instrument addressing protected areas, and supporting and fostering national and multilateral efforts in a comprehensive manner. The Convention defines protected area as "a geographically defined area which is designated or regulated and managed to achieve specific conservation objectives". National protected area systems have been developed and maintained as key elements of national strategies to conserve biological diversity.

Biodiversity Action Plan is an internationally recognized program addressing threatened species and habitats, which is designed to protect and restore biological systems. The original impetus for these plans derives from the 1992 Convention on Biological Diversity (CBD). As of 2006, 188 countries have ratified the CBD, but only a fraction of these have developed substantive BAP documents. The principal elements of a BAP typically include: (a) preparing inventories of biological information for selected species or habitats; (b) assessing the conservation status of species within specified ecosystems; (c) creation of targets for conservation and restoration; and (d) establishing budgets, timelines and institutional partnerships for implementing the BAP.

Key elements of ecological networks

(i) A focus on conserving biodiversity at the ecosystem, landscape or regional scale.

(ii) An emphasis on maintaining or strengthening ecological coherence, primarily through providing for ecological interconnectivity.

(iii) Ensuring that critical areas are buffered from the effects of potentially damaging external activities.

(iv) Restoring degraded ecosystems where appropriate.

(v) Promoting complementarity between land uses and biodiversity conservation objectives, particularly by exploiting the potential biodiversity value of associated semi-natural landscape.

The concept of biodiversity needs to be well understood at the regional level — what it is, what can be done to protect or recover values, and what benefits can be expected from investment in management. This enables to take sound decisions on priorities for investment and management. There is a need to clarify the benefits derived from biodiversity conservation, and to develop the market base for those benefits. National biodiversity values and threatening processes are identified under the Environment Protection and Biodiversity Conservation Act, as matters of national environmental significance.

Regions need to plan to achieve landscape-scale outcomes for biodiversity conservation. Effective cooperation and communication is required between a range of agencies and other bodies, supported by coordinated mapping and information at appropriate scales and, appropriate networks, and sound decision-making tools. Effective regional planning requires both science-based biodiversity information and local knowledge and expertise. Information needs to be in a form appropriate for landscape-scale planning and management.

Regional organizations are required to set biodiversity targets and incorporate them in their regional plans. Regions will differ in their capacity to set, implement, and measure performance against the targets. Regions can build capacity by providing resources, information, facilitation, technical support, skills and training. Support required will vary over time, and based on the situation of the group. A mix of motivational, financial and regulatory mechanisms is best. Strong leadership is a key factor in ensuring mechanisms and are developed and adopted effectively. There are a number of factors that drive effective incorporation of biodiversity conservation in regional planning. The key drivers of effective biodiversity planning and action are leadership, providing consistent and appropriate support, providing information that is relevant and available, building on success, appropriate application of science, effective partnership arrangements, identifying biodiversity values, rewarding private effort to protect public values and encouraging private investment.

For achieving overall economic development, an integration of natural resources, human resources and capital is necessary. The principal objective of regional planning is to maximize resource development potential by maximizing national output. This can be possible only through the optimum utilization of resources in the short-term and sustainable utilization of resources in the long-term. Planning for sustainable development involves the following major principles :

1. Resources must be exploited in an economical manner. This would help minimize waste of resources and also to convert the waste products into economically viable by-products. Technological upgradation is needed to achieve such a goal.
2. Society has to be aware enough to conserve renewable resources and also to conserve non-renewable resources.
3. Multi-purpose use of resources can prevent loss of resources. With scientific advancements, newer applications of resources have proved to be extremely beneficial for the human civilization.
4. Integrated planning is important for the development of economy in a sustainable manner.

5. Industrial locations should be planned in economically viable regions.
6. Prevention of environmental hazards such as pollution created by automobiles, industries, is important for the developmental aspect of planning.

It is extremely important for planners to consider the ecological aspect for our future survival. A concrete database of ecological resources should be prepared by conducting extensive field surveys and using remote sensing technology.

The convention recognized for the first time in international law that the conservation of biological diversity is "a common concern of humankind" and is an integral part of the development process. The agreement covers all ecosystems, species and genetic resources. It links traditional conservation efforts to the economic goal of using biological resources sustainably. It sets principles for the fair and equitable sharing of the benefits arising from the use of genetic resources, notably those destined for commercial use. It also covers the rapidly expanding field of biotechnology through its Cartagena Protocol on Biosafety, addressing technology development and transfer, benefit-sharing and biosafety issues. Importantly, the Convention is legally binding; countries that join it are obliged to implement its provisions.

The convention reminds decision-makers that natural resources are not infinite and sets out a philosophy of sustainable use. While past conservation efforts were aimed at protecting particular species and habitats, the Convention recognizes that ecosystems, species and genes must be used for the benefit of humans. However, this should be done in a way and at a rate that does not lead to the long-term decline of biological diversity.

The convention also offers decision-makers guidance based on the precautionary principle that where there is a threat of significant reduction or loss of biological diversity, lack of full scientific certainty should not be used as a reason for postponing measures to avoid or minimize such a threat. The Convention acknowledges that substantial investments are required to conserve biological diversity. It argues, however, that conservation will bring us significant environmental, economic and social benefits in return.

International Bodies Established by the Convention

The convention's governing body is the Conference of the Parties (COP), consisting of all governments (and regional economic integration organizations) that have ratified the treaty. This ultimate authority reviews progress under the Convention, identifies new priorities, and sets work plans for members. The COP can also make amendments to the Convention, create expert advisory bodies, review progress reports by member nations, and collaborate with other international organizations and agreements.

The Conference of the Parties uses expertise and support from several other bodies that are established by the Convention. In addition to committees or mechanisms established on an ad-hoc basis, two main organs are:

The CBD Secretariat: Based in Montreal, it operates under the United Nations Environment Programme. Its main functions are to organize meetings, draft documents, assist member governments in the implementation of the programme of work, coordinate with other international organizations, and collect and disseminate information.

The Subsidiary Body on Scientific, Technical and Technological Advice: This body is composed of experts from member governments competent in relevant fields. It plays a key role in making recommendations to the COP on scientific and technical issues.

Biodiversity is defined as the variety and variability among living organisms and the ecological complexes in which they occur. It is measured at three levels – the gene, the species and the ecosystem. Forest is a key element of our terrestrial ecological systems. They comprise tree-dominated vegetative associations with an innate complexity, inherent diversity, and serve as a renewable resource base as well as habitat for a myriad of life forms. Forests render numerous goods and services, and maintain life-support systems so essential for life on earth. In ecological lines, it is the diversity of durable interactions among species; it is also related to their immediate environment and their eco-region. In each ecosystem, living organisms are part of a whole, interacting with not only other organisms, but also with the air, water, and soil that surround them. Biodiversity is measured in terms of Alpha, Beta and Gamma diversity.

Alpha diversity refers to diversity within a particular area, community or ecosystem, and is measured by counting the number of taxa within the ecosystem. Beta diversity is species diversity between ecosystems – it involves comparing the number of taxa that are unique to each of the ecosystems. Gamma diversity is a measure of the overall diversity for different ecosystems within a region.

Conversion, destruction and fragmentation of habitat are the single greatest threats to biodiversity. Humans have dramatically transformed landscapes to accommodate our needs for housing, transportation, food, fiber, recreation, and a host of other uses. Even places that provide open space, like parks, refuges or wilderness areas, may have diminished habitat value because of inadequate management, over-use, invasion by harmful exotic species, or contamination from external sources. Most of the species extinctions from 1000 AD to 2000 AD are due to human activities, in particular destruction of plant and animal habitats. Raised rates of extinction are being driven by human consumption of organic resources, especially related to tropical forest destruction. While most of the species that are becoming extinct are not food species, their biomass is converted into human food when their habitat is transformed into pasture, cropland, and orchards. It is estimated that more than 40% of the Earth's biomass is tied up in only the few species that represent humans, livestock and crops. Because an ecosystem decreases in stability as its species are made extinct. The global ecosystem is destined for collapse if it is further reduced in complexity. Factors contributing to loss of biodiversity are over-population, deforestation, pollution and global warming or climate change, driven by human activity. Some characterize loss of biodiversity not as ecosystem degradation but by conversion to trivial standardized ecosystems. In some countries, lack of property rights or access regulation to biotic resources necessarily leads to biodiversity loss. The biodiversity and genetic diversity are dependent upon each other that diversity within a species is necessary to maintain diversity among species, and vice versa. If any one type is removed from the system, the cycle can break down, and the community becomes dominated by a single species.

Conservation of Biodiversity

Biotic resources refer to the plant, animal and microbial resources. They include genetic resources, organisms or parts thereof, populations or any other biotic component of ecosystems with actual or potential use or value for humanity. They are important components for progress and economic activities of any nation. Bioresources management and utilization for human welfare is very important for the optimum utilization of the bioresources.

Rapidly expanding human populations and resource consumption now threaten the biological diversity at three levels: species diversity, genetic diversity and ecosystems diversity. Biological resources are diminished or destroyed in a number of ways. Natural changes in the environment eliminate once successful species or reduce their numbers to mere remnant populations. Humans disrupt ecosystems and extirpate species, both deliberately and accidentally.

The conservation of biological diversity has become a global concern. Although not everybody agrees on extent and significance of current extinction, most consider biodiversity essential. There are basically two main types of conservation options, *in-situ* conservation and *ex-situ* conservation.

In-situ conservation means "on-site conservation". It is the process of protecting an endangered plant or animal species in its natural habitat, either by protecting or by defending the species from predators. The benefit to *in-situ* conservation is that it maintains recovering populations in the surroundings where they have developed their distinctive properties. As a last resort, *ex-situ* conservation may be used on some or all of the population, when *in-situ* conservation is too difficult or impossible.

Wildlife conservation is mostly based on *in situ* conservation. This involves the protection of wildlife habitats. Also, sufficiently large reserves are maintained to enable the target species to exist in large numbers. The population size must be sufficient to enable the necessary genetic diversity to survive within the population, so that it has a good chance of continuing to adapt and evolve overtime. This reserve size can be calculated for target species by examining the population density in naturally-occurring situations. The reserves must then be protected from intrusion or destruction by man and against other catastrophes.

Ex-situ conservation literally means "off-site conservation". It is the process of protecting an endangered species of plants or animals by removing part of the population from a threatened habitat and placing it in a new location, which may be a wild area or within the care of humans. While *ex-situ* conservation comprises some of the oldest and best known conservation methods, it also involves newer, sometimes controversial laboratory methods. Normally, the best method of maximizing a species chance of survival is by relocating part of the population to a less threatened location. It is extremely difficult to mimic the environment of the original colony location given the large number of variables defining the original colony such as microclimate, soils, symbiotic species, absence of severe predation, etc. It is also technically challenging to uproot in the case of plants or trap in the case of animals the required organisms without undue harm.

Endangered plant species may also be preserved in part through seed banks or germ plasm banks. The term seed bank sometimes refers to a cryogenic laboratory facility in which the seeds of certain species can be preserved for up to a century or more without losing their fertility. It can also be used to refer to a special type of arboretum where seeds are harvested and the crop is rotated. For plants that cannot be preserved in seed banks, the only other option for preserving germ plasm is *in-vitro* storage, where cuttings of plants are kept under strict conditions in glass tubes and vessels.

Endangered animal species are preserved using similar techniques. The genetic information needed in the future to reproduce endangered animal species can be preserved in gene banks, which consist of cryogenic facilities used to store living sperm, eggs, or embryos.

India in its geographical area includes 1.8% of forest area according to the Forest Survey of India. The forests cover an actual area of 63.73 million ha (19.39%) and consist of 37.74 million ha of dense forests, 25.51 million ha of open forest and 0.487 million ha of mangroves, apart from 5.19 million ha of scrub and comprises 16 major forest groups (Ministry of Environment and Forests 2002).

India has a rich and varied heritage of biodiversity covering ten biographical zones, the trans-Himalayan, the Himalayan, the Indian desert, the semi-arid zone(s), the Western Ghats, the Deccan Peninsula, the Gangetic Plain, North-East India, and the islands and coasts. India is rich at all levels of biodiversity and is one of the 12 mega diversity countries in the world. India's wide range of climatic and topographical features has resulted in a high level of ecosystem diversity encompassing forests, wetlands, grasslands, deserts, coastal and marine ecosystems, each with a unique assemblage of species. Surveys conducted so far in India have inventoried over 47,000 species of plants and over 89,000 species of animals over just 70% of the country's total area. India's bio-geographical location at the junction of the Agro-tropical, Indo-Malayan and Paleo-Arctic realms has contributed to the biological richness of the country. The endemism of Indian biodiversity is high – about 33% of the country's recorded flora is endemic to the country and is concentrated mainly in the North-East, Western Ghats, North-West Himalaya and the Andaman and Nicobar Islands. About 62% of the known amphibian species and 50% of the lizards are endemic to India, the majority occurring in the Western Ghats. Genetic diversity comprising native species and land races is concentrated in the areas of the Western Ghats, Northern Himalayas, Southern plateau, Central India and North-western Himalayas.

India's rich biodiversity needs to be preserved and the immediate task will be to devise and enforce time-bound plans for saving the habitats of biological resources. Action for conservation must be directed to:

- Intensification of surveys and inventorization of biological resources in different parts of the country including the island ecosystems. The survey should include information on the distribution pattern of participating species/population/communities and the status of ethno biologically important groups.

- Conservation of biodiversity through a network of protected areas including Biosphere Reserves, Marine Reserves, National Parks, Sanctuaries, Gene Conservation Centers, Wetlands, Coral Reefs and such other natural habitats of biodiversity. This should include taxonomic and ecological studies on the flora and fauna with adequate emphasis placed on the lower vertebrate, invertebrate and micro-flora which are important in contributing to the healthy maintenance of ecosystems.
- Full and correct rehabilitation of rural poor/tribals displaced due to creation of national parks/biosphere reserves/tiger reserves.
- Conservation of micro-fauna and micro-flora which help in reclamation of wastelands and revival of biological potential of the land.
- Protection and sustainable use of plant and animal genetic resources through appropriate laws and practices.
- Protection of domesticated species/varieties of plants and animals in order to conserve indigenous genetic diversity.
- Maintenance of corridors between national parks, sanctuaries, forests and other protected areas.
- Emulation and support for protection of traditional skills and knowledge and knowledge for conservation.
- Development of methodologies to multiply, breed and conserve the threatened and endangered species

through modern techniques of tissue culture and biotechnology.

- Discouragement of monoculture and plantation of dominating and exotic species in areas unsuited for them and without sufficient experimentation.
- Restriction on introduction of exotic species of animals without adequate investigation.
- Devising ways and means by which local people can conserve and use thereafter the resources of the common lands and degraded forests, so that they have a stake in the continuing productivity of the resources.
- Encouraging private individuals and institutions to regenerate and develop their wastelands.
- Raising of fuel wood species and provisions of alternatives to reduce dependence on fuel wood.
- Taking measures to increase the productivity of fodder and grasses to bridge the side gap between supply and demand.
- Raising of bamboo and species providing small timber for local house construction and agricultural implements.
- Increasing biomass to meet essential requirement of biomass-based industry.
- Promoting direct relationship between forest-based industry and farmers to raise needed raw materials provided this does not result in the diversion of prime agricultural lands and displacement of small and marginal farmers.
- Extensive research and development in forestry for better regeneration and improved productivity.

- Development of technologies for enhancing the productivity and efficiency of use of all biomass resources.
- Institutional and technological systems to enable rural artisans to sustain biomass based crafts and
- Curtailment of the supply of subsidized biomass resources to industrial consumers.

Protected Areas Network: The protection of wildlife has a long tradition in Indian history. Wise use of natural resources was a prerequisite for many hunter-gatherer societies which date back to at least 6000 BC. Extensive clearance of forests accompanied the advance of agricultural and pastoral societies in subsequent millennia, but an awareness of the need for ecological prudence emerged and many so-called pagan nature conservation practices were retained. As more and more land became settled or cultivated, so these hunting reserves increasingly became refugees for wildlife. Many of these reserves were subsequently declared as national parks or sanctuaries, mostly after Independence in 1947. Examples include Gir in Gujarat, Dachigam in Jammu and Kashmir, Bandipur in Karnataka, Eravikulum in Kerala, Shivpuri in Madhya Pradesh, Simlipal in Orissa, and Kolaedo, Ranthambore and Sariska in Rajasthan.

Wildlife, together with forestry, has traditionally been managed under a single administrative organization within the forest departments of each state or union territory, with the role of central government being mainly advisory. There have been two recent developments. First, the Wildlife (Protection) Act has provided for the creation of posts of chief wildlife wardens and wildlife wardens in the States to exercise statutory powers under the Act. Under this Act, it is also mandatory for the States to set up State Wildlife Advisory Boards. Secondly, the inclusion of protection of wild animals and birds in the concurrent list of the constitution has provided the Union Government with some legislative control over the States in the conservation of wildlife. All states and union territories have set up wildlife wings for national parks or sanctuaries.

The adoption of a National Policy for Wildlife Conservation in 1970 and the enactment of the Wildlife (Protection) Act in 1972 led to a significant growth in the protected areas network. The network was further strengthened by a number of national conservation projects, notably Project Tiger, initiated in April 1973 by the Government of India with support from WWF, and the Crocodile Breeding and Management Project, launched on 1 April, 1975 with technical assistance from United Nations Development Programme and Food and Agriculture Organization.

The Ministry of Environment and Forests is also the focal point for implementation of the Convention on Biological Diversity. The mandates of the Ministry *inter-alia* include survey of flora, fauna, forests and wildlife, and conservation of natural resources. The Biodiversity Bill is an important mechanism for regulating access to biological resources and in establishing benefit-sharing arrangements. The legislation primarily addresses the issue concerning access to genetic resources and associated knowledge by individuals, institutions or companies, and equitable sharing of benefits arising out of the use of these resources and knowledge to the country and the people. The legislation provides for setting up of a three-tiered structure at national, state and local level. A major advancement for the cause of biodiversity conservation in the country and in compliance with requirement of the Convention on Biological Diversity is the drafting of the country's National Biodiversity Strategy and Action Plan (NBSAP) with funding support from the Global Environmental Facility. The strategy and action plan are very broad in scope and comprehensive in coverage and propose to prepare detailed action plans at sub-state, state, regional and national levels based on the framework Policy and Action Strategy on Biodiversity. NBSAP is India's biggest planning and development process aiming at conservation and sustainable use of biological diversity. India has enacted an umbrella legislation called the Biodiversity Act, 2002 and also notified the Biological Diversity Rules, 2004.

Biological Diversity Act - 2002

After an extensive and intensive consultation process involving the stakeholders, the Government of India has brought Biological Diversity Act, 2002.

1. To regulate access to biological resources of the country equitable share in benefits arising out of the use of biological resources.
2. To conserve and sustainable use of biological diversity.
3. Setting up of National Biodiversity Authority (NBA), State Biodiversity Board (SBB) and Biodiversity Management Committee's (BMC's).
4. NBA and SBB are required to consult BMCs in decisions relating to bioresource/related knowledge within their Jurisdiction.
5. To respect and protect knowledge of local communities traditional knowledge related to biodiversity.
6. To secure sharing of benefits with local people as conservers of biological resources and holders of knowledge and information relating to the use of biological resources.
7. All foreign nationals/organizations require prior approval of NBA for obtaining biological resources and/or associated knowledge for use.
8. Indian scientists/individuals require approval of NBA

for transferring results of research to foreign nationals/ organizations.

9. Conservation and development of areas of importance from the standpoint of biological diversity by declaring them as biological diversity heritage sites.
10. Protection and rehabilitation of threatened species.
11. Involvement of institutions of State Government in the broad scheme of the implementation of the Biological Diversity Act through constitution of committees.
12. Protect India's rich biodiversity and associated knowledge against their use by foreign individuals and organizations without sharing benefits arising out of such use and check Biopiracy.
13. Indian Industry needs prior intimation to SBB to obtain bioresources. SBB has right to restrict if found to violate conservation and sustainable use and benefit sharing.
14. Provisions for notifying heritage sites by State Government in consultation with local body.
15. Creation of National, State and Local Biodiversity Fund and its use for conservation of biodiversity.
16. Prior approval is needed from NBA for IPRs in any invention in India or outside India on Bioresources.

Values of Biodiversity

Economic values: Biodiversity is recognized as holding value which can be divided into three main areas:

1. Direct economic value-in the provision of products and services such as provision of food, fuel, building materials, medicines, genetic resources for agriculture, etc.

2. Indirect value-where biodiversity brings economic benefits without the need to consume the resource - air and water

purification, waste decomposition, moderation of the Earth's climate, buffering ecosystems against floods and droughts, protecting and maintaining soils, pollination of crop plants, recreation, tourism, ecotourism, natural history films and publications, etc.

3. Ethical value - cultural and aesthetic benefits. Many ecologists believe there are ethical grounds for conservation, and that our physical and mental well-being is intrinsically linked to interactions with biodiversity.

Direct values are many and their availability is closely linked to the existence of any culture, society and civilization. Some direct values are as follows:

1. Monoculture, meaning the lack of biodiversity is a contributing factor to several agricultural disasters in history. Higher biodiversity controls the spread of certain diseases as viruses would need to adapt themselves with every new species.
2. Biodiversity provides food for humans. About 80% of our food supply comes from just about 20 kinds of plants. Humans use at least 40,000 species of plants and animals a day. Although many kinds of animals are utilized as food, again most consumption is focused on a few species. There are also many people in the world who depend on these species for their food, shelter, and clothing. There is vast untapped potential for increasing the range of food products suitable for human consumption, provided that the high present extinction rate can be stopped.
3. A significant proportion of drugs is derived, directly or indirectly, from biological sources; in most cases these medicines cannot presently be synthesized in a laboratory setting. Only a small proportion of the total diversity of plants has been thoroughly investigated for

potential sources of new drugs. Many medicines and antibiotics are also derived from microorganisms.

4. A wide range of industrial materials are derived directly from biological resources. These include building materials, fibers, dyes, resins, gums, adhesives, rubber and oil. There is enormous potential for further research into sustainably utilizing materials from a wider diversity of organisms.

5. Biodiversity provides many ecosystem services that are often not readily visible. It plays a part in regulating the chemistry of our atmosphere and water supply.

6. Biodiversity is directly involved in recycling nutrients and providing fertile soils.

7. Biodiversity has leisure, cultural and aesthetic value. It has inspired musicians, painters, sculptors, writers and other artists. Many cultural groups view themselves as an integral part of the natural world and show respect for other living organisms.

8. Indian coral reefs have a wide range of resources which are of commercial value. Exploitation of corals, coral debris and coral sands is widespread on the Gulf of Mannar and Gulf of Kutch reefs, while ornamental shells and pearl oysters are the basis for reef industry in the south of India. Sea fans and seaweeds are exported for decorative purposes, and there is a spiny lobster fishing industry along the south-east coast, notably at Tuticorin, Madras and Mandapam. Commercial exploitation of aquarium fishes from Indian coral reefs has gained importance only recently and as yet no organized effort has been made to exploit these resources. Reef fisheries are generally at the subsistence level and yields are unrecorded.

9. Five species of marine turtle occur in Indian waters: Green turtle *Chelonia mydas*, Loggerhead *Caretta caretta*, Olive Ridley *Lepidochelys olivacea*, Hawksbill *Eretmochelys imbricata* and Leatherback *Dermochelys coriacea*. Most of the marine turtle populations found in the Indian region are in decline. The principal reason for the decrease in numbers is deliberate human predation. Turtles are netted and speared along the entire Indian coast. In south-east India the annual catch is estimated at 4,000-5,000 animals, with *C. mydas* accounting for about 70% of the harvest. *C. caretta* and *L. olivacea* are the most widely consumed species. *E. imbricata* is occasionally eaten but it has caused deaths and so is usually caught for its shell alone. *D. coriacea* is boiled for its oil which is used for caulking boats and as protection from marine borers.

Valuing Biodiversity

The economic system of any nation is partially blind. It sees somethings and not certain others. It carefully measures and keeps track of the value of those things most important to buyers and sellers such as food, clothing, manufactured goods, work and indeed money itself but its calculations often completely ignore the value of other things that are harder to buy and sell.

The most basic measure of a nation economic performance is Gross National Product (GNP). In calculating GNP, national resources are not depreciated as they are used up. The heavy use of pesticides may ensure that the grain we grow achieves the highest possible short-term profits but the careless and excessive use of pesticides poisons the ground water reservoirs beneath the field. When adding the costs and benefits of growing the grain, the loss of that fresh water resource is simply ignored. The economic value of clean, fresh ground water is not given price value. Developing countries like India cuts hundreds of acres of forest in a single year. The money received from the sale of logs is counted as part of country's income for the year. Everything is calculated and valued according to the benefits but the wear and tear on the forest is not. In fact, nowhere in the calculations the loss of forest is noted in country's GNP. In fact nation's net losses of forest now exceed timber harvests, when the topsoil has eroded, the net value of the timber crop will be reduced by approximately 40%.

Empirical relationship exists between Gross Domestic Product per head and concentrations of industrial pollutants. When GDP per head is low, concentrations of atmospheric pollutants increase as GDP per head increases, but when GDP per head is high, concentrations decrease as GDP per head increases further. This relationship has been christened as the "environmental Kuznets curve". The logic underlying the environmental Kuznets curve is that resource degradation is reversible: degrade all you want now, you can always recover the stock later, because Earth can be relied upon to rejuvenate it. The science of biodiversity has shown this presumption to be false. The presence of ecological thresholds implies that damage to ecosystems can be irreversible.

The accepted formulas of conventional economic analysis contain short-sighted and arguably illogical assumptions about what is valuable in the future as opposed to the present, specifically the standard discount rate that assesses cost and benefit flows resulting from the development of natural resources routinely assumes that all resources belong totally to the present generation. As a result, any value that they have to future generations is heavily discounted when compared to the value of using them up now or destroying them to make way for something else. The effect is to magnify the power of one generation to compromise all future generations.

Biological Monitoring

The objective of monitoring biodiversity change is to have an understanding of what is changing in the ecosystems and why. By integrating long-term information on species trends/cycles with the abiotic data and land-use change information and with the results of other ecosystem research from the same area, a more complete profile of an ecosystem can be prepared, and evidence of change and/or condition documented. This integrated information should be useful for policy making with respect to natural resource management and the conservation of biodiversity.

As a result of population growth, rapid industrial and technological development, urbanization and injudicious planning without due regard to sustainable development, there has been induced a variety of changes in the environment. Human activities induce such changes in the form of pollution that cause widespread damage to the living organisms in the biosphere. The result is the disruption of ecological balance, growing threat to the entire life support system which is rapidly facing extinction.

Biological methods can be successfully applied in predicting the impact of human activities particularly of pollutants well in advance since they present effective and reliable method of evaluating the effect of anthropogenic substances on living organisms. Thus, microbes, plants, animals, cell organelles, organs, individuals, populations, biotic communities and ecosystems show different levels of sensitivity and can be successfully employed as ecological indicators to assess and predict environmental change in a timely manner. Thus organisms, chiefly plant species, communities or even systems serve as a measure or index of the environment. If plants serve as indicators, they are called plant indicators. Every plant is a product of the conditions under which it grows and is therefore, a measurement of environment. Plants are indicators of conditions, processes and uses. Different species of plants serve as indicators of some characteristic types of environmental conditions. Biological methods of monitoring may provide information about the state of environment due to their following characteristic features at different levels.

(i) Microbes, plants and animals have the ability to accumulate a hazardous substance occurring in the environment.

(ii) Life processes of different organisms can be used to evaluate the action of environmental pollution and that of a given pollutant.

(iii) Changes in the pollution of species and in the structure of ecosystem can indicate the level of environmental deterioration.

Biodiversity indicators are information tools, summarizing data on complex environmental issues to indicate the overall status and trends of biodiversity. They can be used to assess national performance and to signal key issues to be addressed through policy interventions and other actions. The development of indicators is, therefore, important for monitoring the status and trends of biological diversity and, in turn, feeding back information on ways to continually improve the effectiveness of biodiversity management programmes. Biodiversity indicators, when used to assess national or global trends, build a bridge between the fields of policy-making and science. Policy makers set the targets and measurable objectives, while scientists determine relevant variables of biodiversity, monitor current state and develop models to make projections of future biodiversity status. Once they are selected, indicators give direction to monitoring and research programmes.

Genetic Pollution

Purebred naturally evolved region-specific wild species that can be threatened with extinction in a big way through the process of genetic pollution ---uncontrolled hybridization, introgression and genetic swamping which leads to homogenization or replacement of local genotypes as a result of either a numerical and/or fitness advantage of introduced plant or animal. Non-native species can bring about a form of extinction of native plants and animals by hybridization and introgression either through purposeful introduction by humans or through habitat modification, bringing previously isolated species into contact. These phenomena can be especially detrimental for rare species coming into contact with more abundant ones where the abundant ones can interbreed with them swamping the entire rarer gene pool creating hybrids thus driving the entire original purebred native stock to complete extinction. Some degree of gene flow may be a normal, evolutionarily constructive process, and all constellations of genes and genotypes cannot be preserved however, hybridization with or without introgression may, nevertheless, threaten a rare species' existence.

In agriculture and animal husbandry, green revolution popularized the use of conventional hybridization to increase yield many folds by creating "high yielding varieties". Often the handful of breeds of plants and animals hybridized originated in developed countries and were further hybridized with local varieties, in the rest of the developing world, to create high yield strains resistant to local climate and diseases. Local governments and industry since have been pushing hybridization with such zeal that several of the wild and indigenous breeds evolved locally over thousands of years having high resistance to local extremes in climate and immunity to diseases, etc. have already become extinct or are in grave danger of becoming so in the near future. Due to complete disuse because of un-profitability and uncontrolled intentional, compounded with unintentional cross-pollination and cross-breeding, formerly huge gene pools of various wild and indigenous breeds have collapsed causing widespread genetic erosion and genetic pollution resulting in great loss in genetic diversity and biodiversity as a whole.

A Genetically Modified Organism is an organism whose genetic material has been altered using the genetic engineering techniques generally known as recombinant DNA technology. Genetic Engineering today has become another serious and alarming cause of genetic pollution because artificially created and genetically engineered plants and animals in laboratories, which could never have evolved in nature even with conventional hybridization, can live and breed on their own and what is even more alarming is that they interbreed with naturally evolved wild varieties. GM crops today have become a common source for genetic pollution, not only of wild varieties but also of other domesticated varieties derived from relatively natural hybridization.

Genetic erosion coupled with genetic pollution is destroying the needed unique genetic base thereby creating an unforeseen hidden crisis which will result in a severe threat to our food security for the future when diverse genetic material will cease to exist to be able to further improve or hybridize weakening food crops and livestock against more resistant diseases and climatic changes.

4

WATER RESOURCES

Water resources are sources of water that are useful or potentially useful to humans. Water is essential for all forms of life, and this is not different for people. Uses of water include agricultural, industrial, household, recreational and environmental activities. Virtually all of these human-uses require fresh water. 88.7% of water on the Earth is salt water, and over two-thirds of fresh water is frozen in glaciers and polar ice caps, leaving only 0.9% available for human-use. Fresh water is a renewable resource, yet the world's supply of clean, fresh water is steadily decreasing.

Sources of Fresh water

Surface water: Surface water is naturally replenished by precipitation and naturally lost through discharge to the oceans, evaporation, and sub-surface seepage. Although the only natural input to any surface water system is precipitation within its watershed, the total quantity of water in that system at any given time is also dependent on many other factors. These factors include storage capacity in lakes, wetlands and artificial reservoirs, the permeability of the soil beneath these storage bodies, the runoff characteristics of the land in the watershed, the timing of the precipitation and local evaporation rates. All of these factors also affect the proportions of water lost.

Human activities can have a large impact on these factors. Humans often increase storage capacity by constructing reservoirs and decrease it by draining wetlands. Humans often increase runoff quantities and velocities by paving areas and channelizing stream flow.

The total quantity of water available at any given time is an important consideration. Some human water users have an intermittent need for water. For example, many farms require large quantities of water in the spring, and no water at all in the winter. To supply such a farm with water, a surface water system may require a large storage capacity to collect water throughout the year and release it in a short period of time. Other users have a continuous need for water, such as a power plant that requires water for cooling. To supply such a power plant with water, a surface water system only needs enough storage capacity to fill in when average stream flow is below the power plant's need. Nevertheless, over the long-term the average rate of precipitation within a watershed is the upper bound for average consumption of natural surface water from that watershed. Natural surface water can be augmented by importing surface water from another watershed through a canal or pipeline. It can also be artificially augmented from any of the other sources.

Sub-surface water: Sub-surface water, or groundwater, is fresh water located in the pore space of soil and rocks. It is also water that is flowing within aquifers below the water table. Sometimes it is useful to make a distinction between sub-surface water that is closely associated with surface water and deep sub-surface water in an aquifer. Sub-surface water can be thought of in the same terms as surface water: inputs, outputs and storage. The critical difference is that due to its slow rate of turnover, sub-surface water storage is generally much larger compared to inputs than it is for surface water. This difference makes it easy for humans to use sub-surface water unsustainably for a long time without severe consequences. Nevertheless, over the long-term the average rate of seepage above a sub-surface water source is the upper bound for average consumption of water from that source.

The natural input to sub-surface water is seepage from surface water. The natural outputs from sub-surface water are springs and seepage to the oceans. If the surface water source is also subject to substantial evaporation, a sub-surface water source may become saline. This situation can occur naturally under endorheic bodies of water, or artificially under irrigated farmland. In coastal areas, human use of a sub-surface water source may cause the direction of seepage to ocean to reverse which can also cause soil salinization. Humans can also cause sub-surface water to be "lost" (i.e. become unusable) through pollution. Humans can increase the input to a sub-surface water source by building reservoirs or detention ponds.

Water in the ground is in sections called aquifers. Rain rolls down and comes into these. Normally an aquifer is near to the equilibrium in its water content. The water content of an aquifer normally depends on the grain sizes. This means that the rate of extraction may be limited by poor permeability.

Desalination: Desalination is an artificial process by which saline water (generally sea water) is converted to fresh water. The most common desalination processes are distillation and reverse osmosis. Desalination is currently expensive compared to most alternative sources of water, and only a very small fraction of total human-use is satisfied by desalination. It is only economically practical for high-valued uses (such as household and industrial uses) in arid areas. The most extensive use is in the Persian Gulf.

Fresh water during rainy season is stored in the form of reservoirs by constructing a dam across the river or channel. These reservoirs are important for the supply of water for drinking, irrigation, power generation and a number of other uses such as tourism, recreation, etc.

A dam is a barrier that divides waters. Dams generally serve the primary purpose of retaining water, while other structures such as dikes are used to prevent water flow into specific land regions. Most of the first dams were built in Mesopotamia up to 7,000 years ago. These were used to control the water level. The earliest recorded dam is believed to have been on the Sadd Al-Kafara at Wadi Al-Garawi, which is located about 25 kilometers south of Cairo, and built around 2600 B.C. It was destroyed by heavy rain shortly afterwards.

The oldest surviving and standing dam in the world is believed to be the Grand Anicut, also known as the Kallanai, an ancient dam built on the Kaveri River in the state of Tamil Nadu located in southern India. It was built by the Chola King Karikalan, and dates back to the 2nd century AD. Du Jiang Yan in China is the oldest surviving irrigation system which included a dam that directs water flow. It was finished in 251 B.C.

The Kallanai is a massive dam of unhewn stone, over 300 meters long, 4.5 meters high and 20 meters (60 feet) wide, across the main stream of the Cauvery. The purpose of the dam was to divert the waters of the Cauvery across the fertile Delta region for irrigation via canals. The dam is still in excellent repair, and served as a model for later engineers, including the Sir Arthur Cotton's 19th century dam across the Kollidam, the major tributary of the Cauvery. By the early 20th century the irrigated area had been increased to about 1,000,000 acres.

In the Netherlands, a low-lying country, dams were often applied to block rivers in order to regulate the water level and to prevent the sea from entering the marsh lands. Such dams often marked the beginning of a town or city because it was easy to cross the river at such a place, and often gave rise to the respective place's names in Dutch. For instance the Dutch capital Amsterdam (old name Amstelredam) started with a dam through the river Amstel in the late 12th century, and Rotterdam started with a dam through the river Rotte, a minor tributary of the Nieuwe Maas. The central square of Amsterdam, believed to be the original place of the 800 years old dam, still carries the name Dam Square.

Types of Dams

Dams can be formed by human agency, natural causes, or by the intervention of wildlife. Man-made dams are typically classified according to their size (height), intended purpose or structure. By size, international standards define large dams as higher than 15 meters and major dams as over 150 meters in height. By purpose, intended purposes include providing water for irrigation or town or city water supply, improving navigation, creating a reservoir of water to supply industrial uses, generating hydroelectric power, creating recreation areas or habitat for fish and wildlife, flood control and containing effluent from industrial sites such as mines or factories. Few dams serve all of these purposes but some multi-purpose dams serve more than one.

A saddle dam is an auxiliary dam constructed to confine the reservoir created by a primary dam either to permit a higher water elevation and storage or to limit the extent of a reservoir for increased efficiency. An auxiliary dam is constructed in a low spot or saddle through which the reservoir would otherwise escape. On occasion, a reservoir is contained by a similar structure called a dike to prevent inundation of nearby land. Dikes are commonly used for reclamation of arable land from a shallow lake. This is similar to a levee, which is a wall or embankment built along a river or stream to protect adjacent land from flooding.

A check dam is a small dam designed to reduce flow velocity and control soil erosion. Conversely, a wing dam is a structure that only partly restricts a waterway, creating a faster channel that resists the accumulation of sediment.

A dry dam is a dam designed to control flooding. It normally holds back no water and allows the channel to flow freely, except during periods of intense flow that would otherwise cause flooding downstream.

A diversionary dam is a structure designed to divert all or a portion of the flow of a river from its natural course. By structure, based on structure and material used, dams are classified as timber dams, embankment dams or masonry dams, with several subtypes.

Masonry dams: In the arch dam, stability is obtained by a combination of arch and gravity action. If the upstream face is vertical the entire weight of the dam must be carried to the foundation by gravity, while the distribution of the normal hydrostatic pressure between vertical cantilever and arch action will depend upon the stiffness of the dam in a vertical and horizontal direction. When the upstream face is sloped the distribution is more complicated. The normal component of the weight of the arch ring may be taken by the arch action, while the normal hydrostatic pressure will be distributed as described above. The safety of an arch dam is dependent on the strength of the side wall abutments.

Two types of single-arch dams are in use, namely the constant-angle and the constant-radius dam. The constant-radius type employs the same face radius at all elevations of the dam, which means that as the channel grows narrower towards the bottom of the dam the central angle subtended by the face of the dam becomes smaller. A similar type is the double-curvature or thin-shell dam. This method of construction minimizes the amount of concrete necessary for construction but transmits large loads to the foundation and abutments. The appearance is similar to a single-arch dam but with a distinct vertical curvature to it as well lending it the vague appearance of a concave lens as viewed from downstream. The multiple-arch dam consists of a number of single-arch dams with concrete buttresses as the supporting abutments. The multiple-arch dam does not require as many buttresses as the hollow gravity type, but requires good rock foundation because the buttress loads are heavy.

In a gravity dam, stability is secured by making it of such a size and shape that it will resist overturning, sliding and crushing at the toe. The dam will not overturn provided that the moment around the turning point, caused by the water pressure is smaller than the moment caused by the weight of the dam. This is the case if the resultant force of water pressure and weight falls within the base of the dam. However, in order to prevent tensile stress at the upstream face and excessive compressive stress at the downstream face, the dam cross section is usually designed so that the resultant falls within the middle at all elevations of the cross section. For this type of dam, impervious foundations with high bearing strength are essential.

When situated on a suitable site, a gravity dam inspires more confidence in the layman than any other type; it has mass that lends an atmosphere of permanence, stability, and safety. When built on a carefully studied foundation with stresses calculated from completely evaluated loads, the gravity dam probably represents the best developed example of the art of dam building. This is significant because the fear of flood is a strong motivator in many regions, and has resulted in gravity dams being built in some instances where an arch dam would have been more economical. Gravity dams are classified as "solid" or "hollow." Grand Coulee Dam is a solid gravity dam and Itaipu Dam is a hollow gravity dam.

Embankment dams are made from compacted earth, and have two main types, rock-fill and earth-fill dams. Embankment dams rely on their weight to hold back the force of water, like the gravity dams made from concrete.

Rock-fill dams are embankments of compacted free-draining granular earth with an impervious zone. The earth utilized often contains a large percentage of large particles hence the term rock-fill. The impervious zone may be on the upstream face and made of masonry, concrete, plastic membrane, steel sheet piles, timber or other material. The impervious zone may also be within the embankment in which case it is referred to as a core. In the instances where clay is utilized as the impervious material the dam is referred to as a composite dam. To prevent internal erosion of clay into the rock-fill due to seepage forces, the core is separated using a filter. Filters are specifically graded soil designed to prevent the migration of fine grain soil particles. When suitable material is at hand, transportation is minimized leading to cost savings during construction. Rock-fill dams are resistant to damage from earthquakes. However, inadequate quality control during construction can lead to poor compaction and sand in the embankment which can lead to liquefaction of the rock-fill during an earthquake. Liquefaction potential can be reduced by keeping susceptible material from being saturated, and by providing adequate compaction during construction.

Earth-fill dams, also called earthen, rolled-earth or simply earth dams, are constructed as a simple embankment of well compacted earth. A homogeneous rolled-earth dam is entirely constructed of one type of material but may contain a drain layer to collect seep water. A zoned-earth dam has distinct parts or zones of dissimilar material, typically a locally plentiful shell with a watertight clay core. Modern zoned-earth embankments employ filter and drain zones to collect and remove seep water and preserve the integrity of the downstream shell zone. An outdated method of zoned earth dam construction utilized a hydraulic fill to produce a watertight core. Rolled-earth dams may also employ a watertight facing or core in the manner of a rock-fill dam. An interesting type of temporary earth dam occasionally used in high latitudes is the frozen-core dam, in which a coolant is circulated through pipes inside the dam to maintain a watertight region of permafrost within it.

Siting the dam: The narrow part of a deep river valley is the best place for building a dam. The valley sides serve as natural walls. The primary function of the dam's structure is to fill the gap in the natural reservoir line left by the stream channel. The sites are usually those where the gap becomes a minimum for the required storage capacity. The most economical arrangement is often a composite structure such as a masonry dam flanked by earth embankments.

Significant of other engineering and engineering geology considerations when building a dam include:

permeability of the surrounding rock or soil
earthquake faults,
landslides and slope stability,
peak flood flows,
reservoir silting,
environmental impacts on river fisheries, forests and wildlife,
impacts on human habitations,
compensation for land being flooded as well as population resettlement,
removal of toxic materials and buildings from the proposed reservoir area.

Impact is assessed in several ways: the benefits to human society arising from the dam (agriculture, water, damage prevention and power), the harm or benefits to nature and wildlife (especially fish and rare species), the impact on the geology of an area - whether the change to water flow and levels will increase or decrease stability, and the disruption to human lives (relocation, loss of archeological or cultural matters underwater).

Environmental Impacts of Dams

Dams affect many ecological aspects of a river. Dams slow the river and this disturbance may damage or destroy the pattern of ecology. Temperature is another problem that dams create. Rivers tend to have fairly homogeneous temperatures. Reservoirs have layered temperatures, warm on the top and cold on the bottom; in addition often it is water from the colder (lower) layer which is released downstream, and this may have different dissolved oxygen content than before. Organisms depending upon a regular cycle of temperatures may be unable to adapt; the balance of other fauna (especially plant life and microscopic fauna) may be affected by the change of oxygen content. Water exiting a turbine usually contains very little suspended sediment, which can lead to scouring of river beds and loss of riverbanks.

Older dams often lack a fish ladder, which keeps many fish from moving upstream to their natural breeding grounds, causing failure of breeding cycles or blocking of migration paths. Even the presence of a fish ladder does not always prevent a reduction in fish reaching the spawning grounds upstream. In some areas, young fish are transported downstream during parts of the year. A large dam can cause the loss of entire ecosphere, including endangered and undiscovered species in the area, and the replacement of the original environment by a new inland lake. Depending upon the circumstances, a dam can either reduce or increase the net production of greenhouse gases. An increase can occur if the reservoir created by the dam itself acts as a source of substantial amounts of potent greenhouse gases (methane and carbon dioxide) due to plant material in flooded areas decaying in an anaerobic environment. According to the World Commission on Dams Report, when the reservoir is relatively large and no prior clearing of forest in the flooded area was undertaken, greenhouse gas emissions from the reservoir could be higher than those of a conventional oil-fired thermal generation plant. A decrease can occur if the dam is used in place of traditional power generation, since electricity produced from hydroelectric generation does not give rise to any flue gas emissions from fossil fuel combustion (including sulfur dioxide, nitric oxide, carbon monoxide, dust, and mercury from coal).

Drought and its Impacts

A drought is an extended period of months or years when a region notes a deficiency in its water supply. Generally, this occurs when a region receives consistently below average precipitation. It can have a substantial impact on the ecosystem and agriculture of the affected region. Although droughts can persist for several years, even a short, intense drought can cause significant damage and harm the local economy.

Drought is a normal, recurring feature of the climate in most parts of the world. Having adequate drought mitigation strategies in place can greatly reduce the impact. Recurring or long-term drought can bring about desertification. Recurring droughts in Africa have created grave ecological catastrophes, prompting massive food shortages, still recurring.

Droughts go through three stages. Meteorological drought is brought about when there is a prolonged period with less than average precipitation. Meteorological drought usually precedes the other kinds of drought. Agricultural droughts are droughts that affect crop production or the ecology of the range. This condition can also arise independently from any change in precipitation levels when soil conditions and erosion triggered by poorly planned agricultural endeavors cause a shortfall in water available to the crops. However, in a traditional drought, it is caused by an extended period of below average precipitation. Hydrological drought is brought about when the water reserves available in sources such as aquifers, lakes and reservoirs falls below the statistical average. Like an agricultural drought, this can be triggered by more than just a loss of rainfall.

According to a UN climate report, the Himalayan glaciers that are the sources of Asia's biggest rivers - Ganges, Indus,

Brahmaputra, Yangtze, Mekong, Salween and Yellow - could disappear by 2035 as temperatures rise. Approximately 2.4 billion people live in the drainage basin of the Himalayan rivers. India, China, Pakistan, Bangladesh, Nepal and Myanmar could experience floods followed by droughts in coming decades. Drought in India affecting the Ganges is of particular concern, as it provides drinking water and agricultural irrigation for more than 500 million people. Short-term solutions to global warming also carry with them increased chances of drought.

Generally, rainfall is related to the amount of water vapour in the atmosphere, combined with the upward forcing of the air mass containing that water vapour. If either of these is reduced, the result is drought. The factors of drought include above average prevalence of high pressure systems, winds carrying continental, rather than oceanic air masses, El Nino, deforestation, etc.

Consequences of Drought

Periods of drought can have significant environmental, economic and social consequences. The most common consequences include:

1. Death of livestock
2. Reduced crop yields
3. Wildfires
4. Shortages of water for industrial users
5. Desertification
6. Dust storms, when drought hits an area suffering from desertification and erosion
7. Malnutrition, dehydration and related diseases
8. Famine due to lack of water for irrigation
9. Social unrest

10. Mass migration, resulting in internal displacement and international refugees
11. War over natural resources, including water and food
12. Reduced electricity production due to insufficient available coolant
13. Snakes have been known to emerge and snakebites become more common.

The effect varies according to vulnerability. For example, subsistence farmers are more likely to migrate during drought because they do not have alternative food sources. Areas with populations that depend on subsistence farming as a major food source are more vulnerable to drought-triggered famine. Drought is rarely if ever the sole cause of famine; socio-political factors such as extreme widespread poverty play a major role. Drought can also reduce water quality, because lower water flows reduce dilution of pollutants and increase contamination of remaining water sources.

Drought Mitigation Strategies

1. Drought Monitoring - Continuous observation of rainfall levels and comparisons with current usage levels can help prevent man-made drought.
2. Land use - Carefully planned crop rotation can help to minimize erosion and allow farmers to plant less water-dependent crops in drier years.
3. Rainwater harvesting - Collection and storage of rainwater from roofs or other suitable catchments.
4. Recycled water - Wastewater that has been treated and purified for reuse.
5. Transvasement - Building canals or redirecting rivers as massive attempts at irrigation in drought-prone areas.
6. Water restrictions - Water use may be regulated, particularly outdoors. This may involve regulating the

use of sprinklers, hoses or buckets on outdoor plants, the washing of motor vehicles or other outdoor hard surfaces (including roofs and paths), topping up of swimming pools, and also the fitting of water conservation devices inside the home (including shower heads, taps and dual flush toilets).

Floods

A flood is an overflow of an expanse of water that submerges land. In the sense of "flowing water", the word is applied to the inflow of the tide, as opposed to the outflow or "ebb". It is usually due to the mass of water within a body of water, such as a river or lake, exceeding the total capacity of the body, and as a result some of the water flows outside of the normal perimeter of the body. It can also occur in rivers when the strength of the river is so high; it flows right out of the river channel, usually at corners or meanders. These of course, are not applicable in such instances as sea flooding.

Causes: Floods from the sea can cause overflow or over topping of flood defenses like dikes as well as flattening of dunes. Land behind the coastal defence may be inundated or experience damage. A flood from sea may be caused by a heavy storm (storm surge), a high tide, a tsunami, or a combination thereof. As many urban communities are located near the coast this is a major threat around the world. Many rivers flow over relatively flat land border on broad flood plains.

A flood occurs when an area of land, usually low-lying, is covered with water. The worst floods usually occur when a river overflows its banks. Floods happen when soil and vegetation cannot absorb all the water. The water then runs off the land in quantities that cannot be carried in streams, channels or kept in natural ponds or man-made reservoirs.

Periodic floods occur naturally on many rivers, forming an area known as the flood plain. These river floods usually result from heavy rain, sometimes combined with melting snow, which causes the rivers to overflow their banks. A flood that rises and falls rapidly with little or no advance warning is called a flash flood. Coastal areas are occasionally flooded by high tides caused by severe winds on ocean surfaces, or by tsunami waves caused by undersea earthquakes.

Monsoon rainfalls can cause disastrous flooding in some equatorial countries, such as Bangladesh. Hurricanes have different features which, together, can cause devastating flooding. One is the storm surge (sea flooding as much as 8 metres high) caused by the leading edge of the hurricane when it moves from sea to land. Another is the large amounts of precipitation associated with hurricanes. The eye of a hurricane has extremely low pressure, so sea level may rise a few metres in the eye of the storm. This type of coastal flooding occurs regularly in Bangladesh. In Europe, floods from sea may occur as a result of heavy Atlantic storms, pushing the water to the coast.

Undersea earthquakes, eruption of island volcanoes that form a caldera and marine landslips on continental shelves may all engender a tidal wave called a tsunami that causes destruction to coastal areas. Floods are the most frequent type of disaster worldwide. Thus, it is often difficult or impossible to obtain insurance policies which cover destruction of property due to flooding.

Typical Effects of Floods

Primary effects

1. Physical damage - structures such as buildings get damaged due to flood water. Landslides can also take place.
2. Casualties - people and livestock die due to drowning. It can also lead to epidemics and diseases.

Secondary effects

1. Water supplies - contamination of water; clean drinking water becomes scarce.
2. Diseases - Unhygienic conditions. Spread of water-borne diseases.
3. Crops and food supplies - shortage of food crops can be caused due to loss of entire harvest.

Tertiary/long-term effects

1. Economic- economic hardship, due to temporary decline in tourism, rebuilding costs, food shortage leading to price increase, etc. especially to the poor. Insurance and the finance sectors are immediately affected by the risk of severe weather events.
2. Psychological - loss of loved ones, etc.
3. Flood defences, planning and management.

Benefits of flooding: There are many disruptive effects of flooding on human settlements and economic activities. However, flooding can bring benefits, such as making soil more fertile and providing nutrients in which it is deficient.

5

SHORTAGE OF FOOD, WATER AND ENERGY RESOURCES

Shortage of Food

The worldwide crisis is measurable in the decline of grains of all types produced per capita yearly. To provide every person with a daily diet of their preference with sufficient calories and nutrients would require well over 3 billion tons of grain produced annually. But as of around 1990 less than 1.9 billion tons were being produced yearly and since then world production has declined. An estimated 800 million people are suffering from some degree of malnutrition. Besides, the nearly continent wide food supply crisis in Africa, there are other locations such as Russia and former Soviet bloc nations plunged into crisis. The United Nations Food and Agriculture Organization (FAO) and sister U.N. agencies like the World Bank, the International Monetary Fund (IMF), the General Agreement on Tariffs and Trade (GATT), and the World Trade Organization (WTO) blame hunger on "poverty". Dozens of nations once self-sufficient in many food staples have been forced into food import dependency over the past 30 years or even more. Now neither the food stocks nor the financing exists for their food supplies. The GATT launched the Uruguay Round for free trade in 1986 under the slogan "One World, One Market" which culminated in the creation of 1995 of the World Trade Organization. But the cupboard of the World Market is bare. The private financial interest served by UN, IMF, etc. are making sweeping moves to acquire food stocks for hoarding and to take controlling positions in food commodities production, processing and shipping. On the other hand, the FAO stated that the World's population has outstripped the world's resource base, and demanded that population be cut because it can not be fed. On the political front, food is being used as a weapon by those nations which grow food in surplus reserves.

Supplies of fresh water worldwide are under strain because of population growth, face further threats from pollution and increased demands. Caught between the growing demand for fresh water supplies on one hand and limited and increasingly polluted water supplies on the other, many countries face difficult choices. Disputes over sharing water from river basins have already become a common affair especially in the developing countries. Such disputes between countries may escalate waterways. The water crisis has a great impact on food production. Shortage of water could cap future impr ements in the quality of life such as growing enough cities and industries. This worldwide water crisis calls for a global blue revolution as the Green Revolution for agriculture to conserve and manage fresh water and transform the world into water rich world.

Natural disaster such as bad weather, floods, and droughts are not the causes of the world's food crises. Unnatural disasters caused by years of takedown of agriculture infrastructure under wrong policies and assumptions have been responsible for the shortage of food resources. The problems that led to food shortage in each country vary widely. The measures such as food import and producing more food are being followed to counter the shortage of food resources.

Shortage of Water

Fresh water is vital resource for agriculture, manufacturing, transportation and countless other human activities. In many places, where lack of food threatens human survival it is the lack of water that limits food production. Water also plays a key role in sculpting earth's surface moderating climate and diluting pollutants. The available fresh water amounts to a generous supply that is continuously collected, purified and distributed in the hydrological cycle. This natural recycling and purification process provides plenty of fresh water so long as we do not either overload it with slowly degradable or non-degradable wastes or withdraw it from underground supplies faster than it is replenished.

Water scarcity arises from aridity, drought, desiccation and water stress. Water stress occurs because a combination of a dry climate, occasional drought, poverty, rapid population growth and land degradation interact in a destructive manner. As population increases, more tress are cut, more livestocks are grazed and more over-cultivated land loses topsoil and plant nutrients. The resulting loss of tree cover and vegetation dries out the soil, increases the solar reflectivity of the land and increases the amount of dust in the atmosphere which increases the reflectivity of the atmosphere. The loss of water from vegetation increases reflectivity of sunlight from the bare land and dust laden air warms up the atmosphere, reduces and disperses the clouds and can decrease rainfall. Decreased rainfall results in less amount of water and food as well. Therefore, natural as well as human activities affect water cycle which in turn regulates food production.

Consequences of Water Shortage

Water tables are falling on every continent across the world. In a water scarce world, it would be very difficult to increase grain yields. A severe water shortage could have catastrophic consequences in some developing countries unless global solutions are found soon. Almost a billion people could be living in countries with moderate to severe water shortage caused by climate change, contamination and population growth by the year 2025, according to the World Meteorological Organization. Water shortage may accelerate the threat of famine, malnutrition and endemic hunger. In some countries, lakes and rivers have become receptacles for a vile assortment of wastes such as partially treated municipal sewage, toxic industrial effluents and harmful chemicals leached into surface and ground waters from agricultural activities. All of India's major rivers are badly polluted and they are unable to support fish. In virtually every country, where agricultural fertilizers and pesticides are used they have contaminated ground water aquifers and surface waters. Despite the availability of water in these rivers, they cannot be used for drinking or for growing fish because of pollution. These waters cause serious diseases including malaria, cholera, typhoid and schistosomiasis. Successive droughts due to failure of monsoon rains have amplified water shortage problems in India. Poor farmers in developing countries are facing a lack of access to water for growing food. The rising expense of basic food and water would contribute to rampant malnutrition and diseases in hundreds of millions of poor people. The growing scarcity and competition for water stands as a major threat to future advances in poverty alleviation. Food production would be adversely affected in the semiarid regions such as the Asia's major breadbaskets, the Punjab and the North China plain. Tube-well irrigation in semiarid areas has contributed significantly to the increase in food production and reduction in poverty. But, in such areas, the over exploitation of groundwater poses a major threat to environment, health and food security. Withdrawal of water for irrigation affected the rural household, rural economy and environment in a number of ways. Water scarcity is exemplified by situations such as the need to carry heavy pots of water several kilometres everyday to meet household needs the destitution of farmers who lose their lands or of the landless who lose their jobs because of lack of irrigation water, the loss of wetlands or estuaries because of upstream water depletion, increasing health problems due to water pollution and to a rise in incidence of water borne diseases. The regions of China, India, the Middle East and North Africa face severe water shortage where overexploitation of groundwater has been most pervasive. The groundwater problems have two contradictory aspects. First, there is a rapid drawdown of freshwater aquifers mainly due to the worldwide explosion in the use of wells and pumps for irrigation domestic and industrial water supplies; second, there is the opposite problem of rising water tables of saline and sodic water. Added to these is the pollution of aquifers by toxic elements. Water scarcity limits water supply to wild and domesticated animals. Limitations on water intake depress animal performance quicker and more drastically than any other nutrient deficiency. Further, water quality may affect feed consumption and animal health. In livestock, milk production will be greatly affected because of reduced feed consumption. Groundwater scarcity would also affect plants even those that have roots deep in the soil. Therefore, water scarcity would lead to all sorts of problems not only to human beings but also to plants and animals.

Solutions for Water Shortage

Water is not like oil. There is no substitute. If we continue to take it for granted much of the earth is going to run short of water or food or both. We must understand that fresh water is the liquid that lubricates development and its scarcity will lead to a great variety of problems. A global Blue Revolution is required to conserve and manage fresh water supplies in the face of growing demand and increased pollution as the Green Revolution of the 1960's sought to transform agriculture. Such a method would enable to coordinate responses to water scarcity at local, national and international levels. Such management strategies should include water treatment, improving irrigation efficiency, reusing urban waste water and conserving industrial water-use. At the national level especially in water short regions with dense populations adopting a watershed or river basin management perspective is a needed alternative to uncoordinated water management policies by separate jurisdictions. A comprehensive awareness program should be designed to create awareness among literates and illiterates about the value of water. Reforestation and plantation wherever possible should be taken up to protect groundwater from evaporation and to absorb rain water from run off. Such measures would enhance water accumulation in the ground and in surface water bodies. As the water is the life blood for everything, it should be conserved by all means managed properly and used judiciously.

Human Population and Shortage of Energy Resources

Human society has progressed as it has learnt to harness and use more and more energy. Early humans acquired metabolic energy which is necessary for survival by gathering and eating plants. Later, they discovered the use of fire as a source of energy. With this energy source, they started to cook food and to keep warm during winter and for protection against wild animals. Over time, humans learnt to use fire energy to extract metals from ores and to forge tools. In course of time, technological advances made possible improvement in agricultural productivity and the harnessing of water and wind power. These technological advances gradually made humans to use more and more amount of energy. The use of energy has increased many-fold in recent times because of the development of elite technology which made possible the comfortable lifestyle.

All parts of the world have not experienced the dramatic and widespread growth in energy use. There are striking disparities in the sources and amounts of energy used in different parts of the world. The energy consumption is very high in the developed world while there is shortage of energy in the developing countries. In most developing countries modern commercial sources of energy are used largely by the industrial and transport sectors in urban areas. In rural areas, people continue to rely on traditional fuels such as firewood, animals and plant waste, charcoal and an animal and human muscle power. Solar energy is used widely for drying clothes, fish, grain, etc. Many tasks are performed outdoors during daylight hours to make use of sunlight. The urban and rural patterns of energy consumption are significantly different. In India, the energy requirement is increasing sharply because of rapid industrialization, mechanization, urbanization, economic growth, population growth and changing lifestyles and aspirations of the people. The supply of energy has not been able to keep pace with the rising demand. In effect, we are experiencing energy shortages of petrol, electricity, cooking gas, kerosene and fuel wood in our everyday lives.

Commercial and Non-commercial Energy Resources

In India, one-third of the energy used comes from non-commercial sources. The rural population which accounts for almost three-fourths for the country's total population is largely dependent on non-commercial sources for most of its energy needs. The large number of non-motorized vehicles such as bicycles, cycle rickshaws, hand-carts, animals carts, etc. on the roads of our towns and cities reflects the huge dependence on non-commercial sources in urban areas as well. Half of the total energy is consumed by households mainly for cooking food.

Accurate records of use of non-commercial energy sources such as biomass fuels, sunlight and animate power do not exist. Firewood continues to be the major fuel for cooking energy in the country. A substantial amount of fuel wood is consumed by the dead. Over 70 lakh dead bodies are cremated every year in

India. These bodies consume about 30 lakh tonnes of wood annually. While firewood is the preferred biomass fuel, the dependence on different bio-fuels varies from region to region due to vast ecological diversity. Local climate vegetation type and firewood availability often determine the nature of biomass use. In agriculturally prosperous areas, firewood accounts for a lower proportion of the total household energy consumption than in agriculturally poorer areas. This is because the agricultural areas are rich in crop residues and used directly as fuel or fed to cattle resulting in increased availability of cow dung as fuel. In ecologically fragile regions such as deserts, hills and mountains, where it is important to protect the forest cover people's dependence on firewood tend to be much greater.

The commercial energy sources used in India include coal, oil, natural gas, hydroelectric power and nuclear power. The largest source used is coal. It provides about 40% of India's total energy requirements and is the source of our country's commercial energy. Oil accounts for about 35% of the nation's commercial energy supply. India rapidly developed its oil resources to meet the rising demand and reduce its dependence on oil from their countries most of which are politically unstable. India still has to import half of the total requirement of crude oil and oil imports continue to be a heavy drain on the exchequer. Natural gas meets nearly 10% of India's current commercial needs. The current production of natural gas far exceeds the country's ability to transport it to where it could be used. As a result, a large percentage of gas produced is flared at source. Hydroelectric power supplies about 16% of nation's commercial energy. Nuclear power supplies only 2% of commercial energy. In recent years, wind power is given some priority because of its eco-friendly status. Further, it also has several other advantages over coal, oil, gas hydroelectric power and nuclear power. As on today, the percentage of wind power supply to our country's commercial energy is negligible.

Energy Consumption Pattern

The developing countries represent dual society characterized by dichotomies. As a member of developing countries, India is also characterized by dichotomized dual society in respect of energy use which is marked by three sets of contrasts : (1) modern-traditional sector (2) rich-poor and (3) urban-rural.

The modern-traditional sector contrast

Modernization means mechanization and high productivity and applies to all sector of the economy such as industrial, agricultural, transport, commercial and residential. The modern sector demands high input of commercial energy. In India, industrial sector is the largest user of commercial energy followed by transport and commerce. Traditional sectors of our nation's economy such as traditional, agricultural and rural transportation continue to depend heavily on non-commercial sources of energy.

The rich-poor contrast

The life styles, aspirations and consumption patterns of the rich in India and other developing countries are very similar to those of people in the industrialized countries, so is their pattern of energy consumption. In India the poorest consume less than half of the energy consumed by the richest. While the rich have greater access to the more convenient and efficient commercial energy sources such as electricity for lighting and LPG for cooking, the poor depend primarily on firewood for cooking and heating bath water and on kerosene for lighting. Further, the rich have a large catchment's area for acquiring energy and other resources but the poor have to depend upon only locally available energy resources. Therefore, the poor are more directly and immediately affected by a decline in the quality or availability of or access to local resources.

The urban-rural contrast

Commercial energy consumption is very high in towns and cities. Also there is a large demand for high quality fuels and electricity in urban areas. The transport, commercial construction and service sectors in urban areas are dependent largely on commercial energy. Non-commercial sources of energy also contribute to these sectors in urban areas in India. The decision making elite live in urban areas and in effect, there is a preferential flow of energy to these areas.

In India, rural people rely heavily on traditional biomass fuels especially on non-commercial firewood. In rural areas, the domestic sector is the main consumer of energy. Energy use here is characterized by low efficiency of fuels and of the devices used. The chief source of mechanical energy used in agriculture, transportation and domestic chores is animate energy from human and animal muscle power. The commercial energy is used mainly for lighting. Therefore, the urban people rely heavily on commercial energy while rural people on non-commercial energy.

Shortage of Energy Resources

Shortage of energy resources is a result of a variety of factors. Our country suffers from energy shortages like all other developing countries. The rising fuel wood prices and the dependence of the poor on low quality crop residues and cattle dung are the best indications of shortage of fuel wood. In recent years, shortages of coal and electricity have steadily worsened largely because the lower energy prices set by the government do not provide adequate returns or incentives to producers of energy. The persistent shortages of coal and power supply have contributed to a more rapid rise in the consumption of petroleum products. The rapid and unconstrained growth of cities, inadequate public transport and increase in income levels have led to a phenomenal growth in the number of privately owned vehicles. In effect, there is a significant demand for petrol and motor oil. India is meeting this demand by importing oil as well as developing its own oil resources. The import requirement to meet such an ever increasing demand is most likely to show a disastrous effect on India's foreign exchange situation and its external debt. Further, India's economy would continue to be vulnerable to the volatility of the international oil market and of the political situation in the oil producing countries.

India follows development policies which equate development with growth and economic growth with increased consumption of commercial energy. Energy planning does not involve the crucial aspects of the lives of the rural and urban poor, their basic human needs, their settlements, their fuels, the end uses and their energy using devices. The energy planning in essence over-emphasized the energy supplies of the elite.

The decline in the availability of firewood is driving the landless poor and marginal farmers who cannot get adequate crop wastes from their small land holdings to depend on cattle dung. The adoption of domestic biogas plants by many of the larger farmers and cattle owners has deprived the poor of cow dung which they were earlier free to collect from streets and fields for fuel. In many parts of rural India, dung and agricultural wastes are increasingly becoming market commodities. This has been affecting the rural poor and intensifying inequities in access to and distribution of energy resources. These inequities also affect men and women unequally as poor rural women have to bear the increased burden of spending longer hours and more energy searching for and gathering fuel. The millions of poor women are caught in a vicious energy cycle - they eat food to get human energy and then spend all of this energy in producing food and collecting the energy needed to cook it. The scarcity of firewood and other biomass fuels and the increase in the time spent on gathering them reduces the time available for other tasks such as cooking. This in turn can affect the choice of foods. In some urban slums, the shortage of firewood resulted in shifting from slow cooking more nutritious food to quick cooking less nutritious food. The decline in nutritional intake makes people particularly the women who traditionally eat the last and the least in the household, more vulnerable to diseases.

The combination of using inefficient fuel, in inefficient stoves is negative from the standpoints of energy, health of the cook and the environment. Such a combination requires a greater quantity of fuel for cooking meal and exposes the cook to more pollutants. Widespread inefficiency in power generation, transmission, management and use intensifies energy shortages. The transport sector is characterized by inefficiencies. Subsidies by the government that keep energy prices artificially low contribute to energy inefficiencies. These subsidies have led to the wasteful use of energy sources and contributed to energy shortages.

Solutions for Energy Shortages

To overcome energy shortages and to improve our energy future we need to take steps to increase energy supplies sustainable and reduce energy demand through efficient use. We should shift towards renewable energy sources that are more equitably distributed, more affordable and less environmentally destructive than fossil fuels. Energy shortage and increasing energy demand can be overcome by using energy less wastefully and more efficiently. Energy shortage can be overcome by saving energy in two ways. 1) Save energy by changing our energy wasting habits and life styles and 2) Save energy by using energy efficient equipment. Change in life-style is more important as modern life style involves mostly wasteful use of energy creating energy shortage problem. Energy efficient equipment drastically cuts the use of energy and it requires less energy to do the same amount of work that the inefficient equipment does with more energy. Energy efficiency must be followed not only in consumption of energy but also in energy generation and distribution. These various measures serve as powerful strategies for dealing with energy use and shortages. These strategies are an essential part of energy conservation. Energy conservation by using, producing, managing and distributing energy more efficiently by developing green product design and clean technologies and materials as well as reduce pollution and adverse environmental impacts by providing incentives for introducing energy saving equipment technologies and practices and by pricing energy more realistically so that it is used less wastefully.

6

Green Revolution and Environment

The world's worst recorded food disaster occurred in 1943 in British-ruled India. Known as the Bengal, an estimated 4 million people died of hunger that year in eastern India. Initially, this catastrophe was attributed to an acute shortfall in food production in the area. When the British left India in 1947, India continued to be haunted by memories of the Bengal Famine. In effect, food security was one of the main items on free India agenda. This awareness led on one hand to the Green Revolution in India and on the other legislative measures to ensure that businessmen would never again be able to hoard food for reasons of benefit. Since 1950, most of the increase in global production has resulted from green revolution. The green revolution has taken place in 1967-68 in India, it changed India's status from a food deficient country to one of the world leading agricultural nations. There are three basic elements in the method of green revolution: continuing expansion of farming areas; double cropping in the existing farmland; and using seeds with improved genetics. But, double cropping is a primary feature of green revolution. Instead of one crop season per year, the decision was made to have two crop seasons per year. The one season per year practice is based on the fact that there is only one natural monsoon per year. Two crop seasons per year concept is based on one natural monsoon and on one artificial monsoon. The latter came in the form of huge irrigation facilities. Therefore, green revolution is a technology package comprising material components of improved high yielding varieties of rice, wheat, millet, corn, irrigation or controlled water supply and improved moisture utilization, fertilizers and pesticides and associated management skills. The green revolution resulted in a record grain output and created plenty of jobs not only for agricultural workers but also industrial workers by the creation of related facilities such as factories and hydro-electric power stations.

Food Problems

Between 1950 and 1984, world grain production almost tripled and per capita production rose by about 40%, helping reduce hunger and malnutrition around the world. Despite these impressive achievements in food production, population growth is outstripping food production and distribution in areas that support 2 billion people. Unless death rates rise sharply, we seem destined to have a population of around 8.5 billion people by 2025. To provide this many people even with a meatless subsistence diet will require doubling food production and distribution up to 2025. African countries largely rely on food imports from developed countries.

In India, despite the magic of green revolution the agricultural output sometimes falls short of demand. It indicates that the green revolution however impressive has thus not succeeded in making India totally and permanently self-sufficient in food. India faced in the recent past and is facing severe drought conditions due to poor monsoon raising questions about whether the green revolution is really a long-term achievement. India has failed to extend the concept of high yield value seeds to all crops or all regions. Nothing like Bengal Famine can happen in India again but it is disturbing to note that even today there are places like Kalahandi (Orissa) where famine-like conditions have been existing for many years and where some starvation deaths have also been reported. Of course, this is due to reasons other than the availability of food in India but the very fact that some people are still starving here brings into question whether the green revolution has failed in its overall social objective though it has been a resounding success in terms of agricultural production.

Food Security

Green revolution guarantees food security but not nutritional and environmental security. Nutritional security is of visual importance for good health and long-life. There are different categories of people underfed, mal-fed and overfed. Underfed category refers to people who cannot grow or buy enough food to meet their basic energy needs. To maintain good health and to resist disease, people need not only a certain number of calories but also food with the proper amounts of protein, carbohydrates, fats, vitamins and minerals. People who are forced to live on a low protein, high carbohydrate diet consisting only of grains such as wheat, rice or corn often suffer from malnutrition deficiencies of protein and other key nutrients. Many of the world's desperately poor people especially children suffer from both under-nutrition and malnutrition. Further, environmental security is the base to carry out any mission to provide food security. Because, good environment caters not only the needs of the people and also the hunger of all wild and domesticated animals. Bad environment coupled with drought conditions in recent times led to fodder shortage for animals in areas like Rajasthan and Bihar. As a result, large scale animal deaths have occurred. It is more so with domesticated animals such as cattle and resulting in meat shortage. Therefore, green revolution mission must include nutritional and environmental security in order to provide food security in real sense to all. Further, the method of green revolution should be applied to all other crops in order to produce surplus yields in grains and other produce.

The green revolution is a success story of post-independence period in increasing food production. In early fifties, our food production was about 50 million tonnes and the population was increasing at an alarming rate. Some western countries had predicted that India would starve but prediction was proved wrong. Taking the food production level into consideration in the light of ever growing population, India has its compulsive need to raise food production. Since the land to man ratio is narrowing rapidly, there is almost no scope for horizontal expansion to meet the demand. This ever growing population of India triggers the transition from traditional practices to modern science based agriculture. Indian agriculture is facing an arduous task to provide food security as well as nutritional security for all.

Introduction of wheat germplasm gave birth to Indian Green Revolution. An increase in food grain production was possible as a result of adoption of quality seeds, higher doses of chemical fertilizers and plant protection chemicals (pesticides), coupled with assured irrigation. The impact of green revolution was so dramatic that India became a model before the world. Our success on food front in short time has received international attention and appreciation but still we have many ways to increase the agricultural production on a sustainable manner. Because, the concept of green revolution is based on the use of chemical fertilizers and pesticides. In other words, our agriculture has become chemicalized. As the availability of land is decreasing day by day, application of fertilizers and pesticides has become necessary to meet the demand for food grains. The effect of prolonged and overuse of chemicals on soil has resulted in human health hazards and pollution of the environment. Therefore the point of sustainability of Indian agriculture has become a real challenge in order to provide food, nutrition and environmental security to human populations.

Chemical Fertilizers

The use of chemical fertilizers is closely linked to the concept of Green Revolution which describes the breakthrough in food grain production and rapid diffusion of the new semi-dwarf wheat and rice varieties in India, Pakistan and other parts of the developing world. This strategy was in the form of a package programme woven around new seeds of high yielding varieties and included other inputs such as adequate irrigation, water supply, chemical fertilizers, plant protection chemicals, and mechanization of agriculture, supply of electricity at subsidized rates, improvement of rural infrastructure, credit and marketing facilities on co-operative basis. The idea was to demonstrate how productivity could be raised without increasing the area under cultivation. It is in this context, chemical fertilizers are of greatest importance to boost agricultural yields without increasing the land area under cultivation.

Composition of chemical fertilizers: The use of chemical fertilizers is aimed at increasing the agricultural production in order to meet the requirements of the continually increasing human and cattle populations. Chemical fertilizers are inorganic fertilizers of a concentrated nature used mainly to restore soil fertility in order to supply essential nutrients to crop plants. The fertilizers are also called as artificial or inorganic manures. The most common nutrients in these fertilizers are nitrogen, phosphorous and potassium. The nitrogen is present in the form of ammonium ions, nitrate ions, or urea; the phosphorous is present in the form of phosphate ions and potassium as potassium ions. Other plant nutrients may also be present in low or trace amounts. Nitrogen fertilizers are divided into four groups according to the manner in which the nitrogen is combined with other elements. They are nitrate, ammonia and ammonium salts, chemical compounds containing nitrogen in the amide form, and plant and animal by-products. Sodium nitrate is a pioneer nitrogenous fertilizer which is directly available to plants. Ammonium sulphate and ammonium nitrate are mixed forms of usable fertilizers and are important particularly for acidic soils. Ammonium chloride is another form of nitrate which is largely used in industries. Urea is a highly concentrated nitrogenous fertilizer and suitable for most crops. It can be applied to all soils. Ammonia is applied directly to the soil from special containers. Its use is very expensive. Calcium ammonium nitrate is a fine free flowering nitrogenous fertilizer and applied to neutral and acidic soils. Phosphate fertilizers are classified as natural phosphates treated or processed phosphates and by-product phosphates and chemical phosphates. Rock phosphate is found in nature but is not used as a fertilizer in India. Super phosphate is the most widely used phosphoric fertilizer and suitable for all crops and applied to all soils. Bone-meal in the form of raw bone-meal and steamed bone-meal is used as phosphate fertilizer. Potassic fertilizers in common use are muriate of potash (potassium chloride) and sulphate of potash (potassium sulphate). These salts are important constituents of water of oceans and inland seas. These potassic fertilizers are applied to any soil. All these forms of chemical fertilizers are produced on commercial basic and sold at high prices. The use of these fertilizers is a necessary evil for higher yields of the crop on a limited parcel of land deficient of plant nutrients. Fertilizer use is clearly an important component in agricultural growth and its potential is greatest where land resources are scarce. The chemical fertilizers are easily transported, stored and applied in proportions suited to the actual requirement of different crops and soils. Throughout the world, their use increased about tenfold.

Environmental Impacts of Chemical Fertilizers

The judicious use of chemical fertilizers increases the agricultural production but poor management results in many undesirable side effects on the environment. These may result from excessive use of fertilizers, unbalanced use of nutrients or even incidental addition of toxic elements as impurities in the fertilizer materials. High levels of nitrate nitrogen content in the surface waters result in eutrophication of water bodies. High concentration nitrate in drinking water has been found to cause methaemoglobinaemia in infants, a fatal disease characterized by cyanosis in which blood pigment loses oxygen required by all human tissues. Human cancer has been associated with nitrate through the formulation of N-nitrosamines and nitrosamides which are extremely powerful carcinogenic agents. Nitrate itself may be carcinogenic without the formation of nitrosamides. There is a positive correlation between nitrate uptake and gastric cancer. In India, cancer cases are rising but no study has been made to identify the possible link between high nitrate content of drinking water and increasing cases of cancer in a population of any particular region. Fertilizers can contribute to eutrophication i.e., promotion of growth of plants, animals and micro-organisms in ponds, lakes and rivers. Nitrogen and phosphorous are the main nutrients involved in this type of pollution. Enrichment with nitrogen and phosphorous causes an increase in the growth of algae and other aquatic weeds, which choke the water ways making water turbid and unpotable. When algae die toxins are produced. The decomposing organic matter reduces oxygen content in water which may decrease or affect fish production. The chemical fertilizers do not add humus to the soil. They cause soil to become compacted and less suitable for crop growth and lower the oxygen content of the soil and prevent added fertilizer from being taken up efficiently. The fertilizers are made up of only a few minerals. They impede the uptake of other minerals and imbalance the whole mineral patterns of plant body. Plants also become less resistant to diseases. Nitrate fertilizers increase the total crop yield by carbohydrates but at the expense of protein. Fertilizers use produces over-sized fruits and vegetables but they are more prone to insects and other pests. Overtime, the accumulation of fertilizer compounds and other substances can lead to lower soil fertility and excessive concentration in the crops cultivated. Green house gas (nitrous oxide) emanates from the chemical fertilizers added to the soil and this gas damages the ozone layer.

Control of Chemical Fertilizer Pollution

The land management practices which decrease detriment run-off should be followed. High losses are likely when fertilizer input exceeds crop requirement. The rate of application should be determined on the basis of soil and crop requirements. There are a number of ways for reducing the nitrate leaching losses. With lighter and more frequent irrigation schedules, nitrate leaching losses can be reduced. Another method suggested to decrease leaching losses of nitrate is the application of balanced nutrients. Such a practice encourages better root and shoot growth. As a result, the plant roots could utilize the applied nutrients better thus reducing leaching losses. It is also possible to minimise losses of nitrogen and phosphorous by keeping the soil covered instead of bare fallow periods so as to reduce run-off losses. Use of organic manures, green manures and recycling of organic wastes can be extremely useful in controlling the nutrient losses and hence the environmental degradation. Organic agriculture is one of the most widely practiced, diversified conventional farming systems to make agriculture sustainable. This system is the most desirable one to maintain good soil health and stability in food grain production to meet the requirement. This system is dubious to the farmers of developing countries. It avoids the use of chemical fertilizers and relies on crop rotation, crop residues, animal manures, legumes, green manures off-farm organic wastes, etc. Until the mid 20th century, organic farming was the way of life and it was not an alternative farming system. Still in many third world countries where the farmers are not able to afford modern agricultural inputs, it is a way of life as much as it is a method of farming. This farming is profitable because of low cost of production though with somewhat lower yields than modern farming. Its success depends on the efficient agronomic management to stimulate the productivity of the soil resource. It is comparatively free from complex problems associated with modern agriculture and eco-friendly as it conserves the natural resources of farming without polluting the atmosphere, soil and water resources. It also enhances the biomass availability to use as a source of renewable energy in rural areas. The principles of organic farming include the following: i) Use nature as the best role model for agriculture, ii) The soil has to be considered as a living system not an inert bowl for unloading chemicals, iii) Farming technique should be based on an intimate understanding of nature's ways, iv) Use of eco-friendly technology based on biological system, and v) Maintenance of soil fertility for optimum production and optimum nutritional value of staple food.

Pesticides

The longest war in human history is our ongoing war against insect pests. This war was declared about 10,000 years ago, when humans first got serious about agriculture and we are not closer to winning today than we were then. In fact, the multitudes of insects that share our fondness for rice and corn, cotton and wheat and beans and apples seem to be gaining on us. Pesticide-use and critical modern input have become an established global practice. Together with synthetic or chemical fertilizers, it is increasingly chemicalizing agricultural production and agro ecosystems. Its place in the yield augmenting package of agricultural practices is only as yield saver for it does not contribute directly to crop yield enhancement. It contributes merely by cutting crop losses caused by insect pests and diseases thereby ensuring a realisable high yield under the farmer's particular agro-climate conditions. The race for higher yields of crops on modern farming has caught the farmers, simultaneously in a race for ever increasing application of pesticides. But these two races namely the emergence of resistant strains among old pests and newer insect pests. Therefore, the emphasis in tackling the loss arising from pest needs a new orientation on the basis of constraints.

Pesticide Usage Trend in India

India is one of the foremost countries in the third world to start large scale use of pesticides for the control of insect pests of public health and agricultural importance. The use of pesticides in India commenced around 1948-49. Originally, some pesticides like DDT were imported but with the passage of time the country progressed well and now there are over 400 chemical factories manufacturing about 60 basic pesticides. Pesticide-use is increasing at 2-5% per annum. Of the total 90,000 tonnes of annual pesticide-usage, only 63% is meant for agricultural purpose and about 1000 crore rupees agro-pesticide market is concentrated in Andhra Pradesh, Karnataka, Gujarat and Punjab accounting for about 3/4 of the sale for use in cotton, paddy, jowar and wheat crops. These crops use 80% of the pesticides sold and fruits and vegetables account for nearly 10%. Of the more than 77,000 pesticide distribution points, more than 70% are owned by private traders in Andhra Pradesh, Tamil Nadu, Uttar Pradesh, Gujarat and West Bengal. The consumption rate of pesticides in Indian agriculture stands at about 400g per hectare which is much below the average rate of consumption of over 1500g per hectare in USA, 2000g/ha in Europe, and 10-12 kgs/ha in Japan. Of the pesticides used, 80% are insecticides, 11% fungicides and 7% herbicides. Up to 1971, the major portion of pesticide production was consumed for non-agricultural purposes. From 1972 onwards, over 70% of total consumption has been used in agricultural sector. The use of pesticides has greatly increased agricultural production and saved millions of lives from insect borne diseases, but the use of certain pesticides has resulted in the pollution of the environment.

Pesticide Types and Uses

A pest is any species that competes with us for food, invades gardens, destroys wood in houses, spreads disease or is simply a nuisance. World wide some 10,000 species of insects attack crops whose yields are also reduced by about 2000 species of weeds and some 1,00,000 plant diseases caused by bacteria, viruses, fungi and algae. In natural ecosystems and many polyculture agro-ecosystems, natural enemies control the populations of pest species. When we simplify natural ecosystems we upset these natural checks and balances that keep any one species from taking over for very long. Then we have to devise ways to protect our monoculture crops, farms and gardens from insects and other pests that nature once controlled at no cost.

We have developed a variety of pesticides to kill organisms which we consider undesirable. Common types of pesticides include insecticides, herbicides, fungicides, nematocides and rodenticides well before 500 B.C; by the 1400s toxic compound of arsenic, lead and mercury were being applied to crops as insecticides. This approach was abandoned in the late 1920s when the increasing number of human poisonings and fatalities encouraged a search for less toxic substitutes. In the 1600s nicotine sulphate extracted from tobacco leaves came into use as an insecticide. In the mid-1800s two more natural pesticides were introduced. One was pyrethrum obtained from the heads of chrysanthemum flowers; the other one was rotenone from the root of the derris plant and other tropical forest legumes. The first generation pesticides were mainly natural substances. The second generation pesticides refer to a major pest control revolution which began in 1939 when Paul Hermann Muller discovered the DDT (dichloro-diphenyl-trichloro-ethane), a chemical known since 1974 was a potential insecticide. It soon became the world's most used pesticide. Since 1945, chemists have developed hundreds of synthetic organic chemicals for use as pesticides. Fungicides are used primarily to treat seeds, to protect fruits, potatoes and vegetables from fungal diseases during growth and after harvest. Some products are coated with wax to give a shiny look and to seal in moisture and slow rotting. Pesticides are added to products as diverse as paints, shampoos, carpets, contact lenses, etc. Some pesticides are broad spectrum agents which are toxic to many species while some others are selective or narrow spectrum agents which are effective against a narrowly defined group of organisms. Pesticides vary in their persistence, the length of time they remain deadly in the environment.

Pesticides save human lives. For example DDT and other chlorinated hydrocarbon and organophosphate insecticides have prevented the premature deaths of millions of people from insect transmitted diseases such as malaria, buonic plague, sleeping sickness, etc. Pesticides increase food supplies and lower food costs. They increase profits for farmers, work faster and better than alternatives. Some consider that the health risks of pesticides are insignificant compared with their health and other benefits. They argue that the reality is that pesticides when used in the approved regulatory manner pose on risk to either farm workers or consumers. Safer and more effective pesticides are being developed worldwide. Scientists continue to search for the ideal pest killing chemicals which would kill only the target pest, harm on other species, disappear or break down into something harming after doing its job, not cause genetic resistance in target organisms and be cheaper than doing nothing.

Harmful Effects of Chemical Pesticides

The contamination of food materials with pesticides is one of the major problems confronting man. The consumer runs the greatest risk of exposure to pesticides through the contaminated food. The intake of pesticides through food and other sources results in their accumulation in the body tissues of human beings. Residents of different countries have been found to contain different levels of DDT. It has been shown that these chemicals can be transferred from the mother to the foetus so that babies may be borne with insecticides in their tissues. Several evils are associated with the widespread use of synthetic pesticides in agriculture. In the long run the multifarious harmful effects of chemical pesticides outweigh their benefits. Increased use of pesticides has caused contamination of soil, air and surface and ground waters besides affecting the crop plants and produce. Acute poisoning is often caused by careless use of these chemicals, long-term exposure affects animal biological system. Carcinogenic, teratogenic and tumorogenic effects are common. BHC (benzene hexa chloride) is widely used in our country to control different crop pests owing to its cheapness and efficacy. Though other chlorinated compounds like DDT, heptachlor, aldrin and chlordane are not that popular they are also recommended for pest control. These cyclic hydrocarbons with chlorine substitutes block ring oxidations and are resistant to biodegradation. They are thus able to thrive for long periods in the environment and accumulate in animals. This persistence along with their animal carcinogenicity has caused concern that exposed humans to cancer risk from these chemicals.

In plants, effects like phytotoxicity, pollen sterility, growth retardation and residues are noticed following the use of certain agro-chemicals. Resistance in insects and mites to pesticides has developed in varying degrees to almost every chemical employed in crop protection. For example, cotton bollworm developed several-fold resistance to many commonly used insecticides due to indiscriminate use of chemicals. Owing to years of exposure many pests have become immune to pesticides. In the field, both the target and non-target insects are developing resistance which may be specific or general to the sprays of chemical pesticides. The biological mechanisms of resistance among insects to pesticide are well-known. For example, certain enzyme secretions by the insects may decompose the pesticides and destroy its killer power. The insect may also develop resistance by altering the rate of penetration of the insecticide or the site of pesticide action. Mites, ticks, fungi and rodents have all shown resistance to one pesticide or the other. Recent studies indicate that pesticide residues that enter through food affect the reproductive system of children in developing countries. Scientists found the DDE, a derivative of DDT in blood mimics the effect of hormone oestrogen causing early puberty and higher risk of developing breast cancer. Experiments conducted on rats indicate that DDE causes the brain to send out the biochemical signals that stimulate puberty. As the banned chemical DDT is still in use in developing countries mainly to control malaria the effect of DDE is of great concern. It has been suggested that children in developing countries do not normally suffer from early puberty because they tend to be under nourished and this slows their development down. But, even if the effect on puberty is masked, their reproductive system could still be harmed. Exposure to chemical contaminants has been found to trigger early genital growth and pubic hair development in boys and enhances the risk of developing testicular cancer. Therefore, the use of chemical pesticides is good for short-term benefits but detrimental in the long run.

Re-examination and Substitutes for Chemical Pesticides

Social awareness of the harmful effects has begun to develop among agricultural scientists, pesticide manufacturing industries and policy makers. But farmers and consumers are by and large unconcerned if not entirely unaware. The prospect of vigorous and sustained movement against chemical pesticides is remote and dim at present. In so far as agricultural scientists are concerned this awareness is abundantly reflected in the latest shift of emphasis from prophylactic use of chemical pesticides to their need based application and integrated pest management strategies. Farmers are now being asked to use chemical pesticides sparingly strictly according to recommendations and only when the pest population has reached the critical size. While gradually reducing the use of chemical pesticides bio-pesticides must be discovered. Further a coherent pest management programme that is environment friendly and able to curtail loss has been developed. This is called integrated pest management strategy. This strategy is defined as an integrated and planned execution of different pest management strategies and actions with the sole objective of reducing losses from pests with minimum ecological implications. Eradication of pest is neither possible nor economical. Keeping this in view, the IPM is to manipulate the populations of pests and their natural enemies in such a way so that the pest population remains below economic threshold levels. IPM comprises of the cultural, mechanical, physical, biological, varietal, pest surveillance and forecasting, chemical and other control methods. Control of pests by using bioagents is of utmost importance to minimise environmental damage. Success of pest control programmes primarily depends upon identification, conservation and enhancement of population of natural enemies which are commonly found along with the pest population in the agro, ecosystems. Recent advances in pest control with bio-agents include biochemical substances like pheromones, insect growth regulators, chemosterilants, etc. Biological control methods are often slow in action and yield at times unpredictable results; they may cost more than the chemical pesticides and may even fail sometimes. Any such failure is only due to lack of knowledge about the population dynamics of general ecology of insect pests. Therefore, a thorough understanding of the general ecology and population dynamics of bio-enemies of pests is essential for the successful implementation of bio-control programmes with rewarding results.

7

Environment Pollution and Solid Waste Management

Pollution is the introduction of pollutants (whether chemical substances, or energy such as noise, heat, or light) into the environment to such a point that its effects become harmful to human health, other living organisms, or the environment.

Air pollution is the modification of the natural characteristics of the atmosphere by a chemical, particulate matter, or biological agent. The atmosphere is a complex, dynamic natural gaseous system that is essential to support life on planet Earth. Stratospheric ozone depletion due to air pollution has long been recognized as a threat to human health as well as to the Earth's ecosystems.

Worldwide air pollution is responsible for large numbers of deaths and cases of respiratory disease. While major stationary sources are often identified with air pollution, the greatest source of emissions is actually mobile sources, mainly automobiles. Gases such as carbon dioxide, which contribute to global warming, have recently gained recognition as pollutants by climate scientists, while they also recognize that carbon dioxide is essential for plant life through photosynthesis.

There are many substances in the air which may impair the health of plants and animals (including humans), or reduce visibility. These arise both from natural processes and human activity. Substances not naturally found in the air or at greater concentrations or in different locations from usual are referred to as pollutants.

Pollutants can be classified as either primary or secondary. Primary pollutants are substances directly emitted from a process, such as ash from a volcanic eruption or the carbon monoxide gas from a motor vehicle exhaust. Secondary pollutants are not emitted directly. Rather, they form in the air when primary pollutants react or interact. An important example of a secondary pollutant is ground level ozone - one of the many secondary pollutants that make up photochemical smog. Note that some pollutants may be both primary and secondary: that is, they are both emitted directly and formed from other primary pollutants.

Major Air Pollutants

Major Air pollutants produced by human activity include:

1. Sulfur oxides (SOx) especially sulfur dioxide is emitted from burning of coal and oil.
2. Nitrogen oxides (NOx) especially nitrogen dioxide are emitted from high temperature combustion. Can be seen as the brown haze dome above or plume downwind of cities.
3. Carbon monoxide is colourless, odourless, non-irritating but very poisonous gas. It is a product by incomplete combustion of fuel such as natural gas, coal or wood. Vehicular exhaust is a major source of carbon monoxide.
4. Carbon dioxide (CO_2), a greenhouse gas emitted from combustion.
5. Volatile organic compounds (VOC), such as hydrocarbon fuel vapors and solvents.
6. Particulate matter (PM), measured as smoke and dust. PM10 is the fraction of suspended particles 10 micrometers in diameter and smaller that will enter the nasal cavity. PM2.5 has a maximum particle size of 2.5 µm and will enter the bronchia and lungs.

7. Toxic metals, such as lead, cadmium and copper.
8. Chlorofluorocarbons (CFCs), harmful to the ozone layer emitted from products currently banned from use.
9. Ammonia NH_3 emitted from agricultural processes.
10. Odors, such as from garbage, sewage, and industrial processes.
11. Radioactive pollutants produced by nuclear explosions and war explosives, and natural processes such as radon.

Secondary pollutants include:

1. Particulate matter formed from gaseous primary pollutants and compounds in photochemical smog, such as nitrogen dioxide.
2. Ground level ozone (O_3) formed from NOx and VOCs.
3. Peroxyacetyl nitrate (PAN) similarly formed from NOx and VOCs.

Minor Air Pollutants

1. A large number of minor hazardous air pollutants. Some of these are regulated in USA under the Clean Air Act and in Europe under the Air Framework Directive.
2. A variety of persistent organic pollutants, which can attach to particulate matter.

Sources of Air Pollution

These sources can be classified into two major categories – anthropogenic and natural. Anthropogenic sources (human activity) mostly related to burning different kinds of fuel.

1. Stationary sources as smoke stacks of power plants, manufacturing facilities, municipal waste incinerators.
2. Mobile sources as motor vehicles, aircraft etc.

3. Combustion-fired power plants.
4. Controlled burn practices used in agriculture and forestry management.
5. Motor vehicles generating air pollution emissions.
6. Marine vessels, such as container ships or cruise ships, and related port air pollution.
7. Burning wood, fireplaces, stoves, furnaces and incinerators.
8. Oil refining, power plant operation and industrial activity in general.
9. Chemicals, dust and crop waste burning in farming.
10. Fumes from paint, hair spray, varnish, aerosol sprays and other solvents.
11. Waste deposition in landfills, which generate methane.
12. Military uses, such as nuclear weapons, toxic gases, germ warfare and rocketry.

Natural sources :

1. Dust from natural sources, usually large areas of land with little or no vegetation.
2. Methane, emitted by the digestion of food by animals, for example cattle.
3. Radon gas from radioactive decay within the Earth's crust.
4. Smoke and carbon monoxide from wildfires.
5. Volcanic activity, which produces sulfur, chlorine and ash particulates.

Indoor Air Quality

A lack of ventilation indoors concentrates air pollution where people often spend the majority of their time. Radon gas, a carcinogen, is exuded from the Earth in certain locations and trapped inside houses. Building materials including carpeting and plywood emit formaldehyde gas. Paint and solvents give off volatile organic compounds as they dry. Lead paint can degenerate into dust and be inhaled. Intentional air pollution is introduced with the use of air fresheners, incense, and other scented items. Controlled wood fires in stoves and fireplaces can add significant amounts of smoke particulates into the air, inside and outside. Indoor pollution fatalities may be caused by using pesticides and other chemical sprays indoors without proper ventilation.

Chronic carbon monoxide poisoning can result even from poorly adjusted pilot lights. Traps are built into all domestic plumbing to keep sewer gas, hydrogen sulfide, out of interiors. Clothing emits tetrachloroethylene, or other dry cleaning fluids, for days after dry cleaning. Though its use has now been banned in many countries, the extensive use of asbestos in industrial and domestic environments in the past has left a potentially very dangerous material in many localities. Asbestosis is a chronic inflammatory medical condition affecting the tissue of the lungs. It occurs after long-term, heavy exposure to asbestos from asbestos-containing materials in structures. Sufferers have severe shortness of breath and are at an increased risk regarding several different types of lung cancer. According to the World Health Organization, these may be defined as asbestosis, lung cancer, and mesothelioma (a rare form of cancer).

Biological sources of air pollution are also found indoors, as gases and airborne particulates. Pets produce dander, people produce dust from minute skin flakes and decomposed hair, dust mites in bedding, carpeting and furniture produce enzymes and micron-sized fecal droppings, inhabitants emit methane, mold forms in walls and generates mycotoxins and spores, air conditioning systems can incubate Legionnaires' disease and mold, and houseplants, soil and surrounding gardens can produce pollen, dust and mold. In Indoors, the lack of air circulation allows these airborne pollutants to accumulate more than they would otherwise occur in nature.

The health effects caused by air pollutants may range from subtle biochemical and physiological changes to difficulty in breathing, wheezing, coughing and aggravation of existing respiratory and cardiac conditions. These effects can result in increased medication use, increased doctor or emergency room visits, more hospital admissions and premature death. The human health effects of poor air quality are far reaching, but principally affect the body's respiratory system and the cardiovascular system. Individual reactions to air pollutants depend on the type of pollutant a person is exposed to, the degree of exposure, the individual's health status and genetics. People who exercise outdoors, for example, on hot, smoggy days increase their exposure to pollutants in the air.

Reduction Efforts

Efforts to reduce pollution from mobile sources includes primary regulation, expanding regulation to new sources (such as cruise and transport ships, farm equipment, and small gas-powered equipment such as lawn trimmers, chainsaws and snowmobiles), increased fuel efficiency (such as through the use of hybrid vehicles), conversion to cleaner fuels (such as bioethanol) or conversion to electric vehicles with renewable energy sources.

Control Devices

The following items are commonly used as pollution control devices by industry or transportation devices. They can either destroy contaminants or remove them from an exhaust stream before it is emitted into the atmosphere.

1. Particulate control

2. Mechanical collectors (dust cyclones, multi-cyclones)
3. Electrostatic precipitators
4. Bag houses
5. Particulate scrubbers
6. Scrubbers
7. Baffle spray scrubber
8. Cyclonic spray scrubber
9. Ejector venturi scrubber
10. Mechanically aided scrubber
11. Spray tower
12. Wet scrubber
13. NOx control
14. Low NOx burners
15. Selective catalytic reduction
16. Selective non-catalytic reduction
17. NOx scrubbers
18. Exhaust gas recirculation
19. Catalytic converter
20. VOC abatement
21. Adsorption systems, such as activated carbon
22. Flares
23. Thermal oxidizers
24. Catalytic oxidizers
25. Biofilters
26. Absorption (scrubbing)
27. Cryogenic condensers
28. Vapor recovery systems
29. Acid Gas/SO_2 control
30. Wet scrubbers
31. Dry scrubbers

32. Flue gas desulphurization
33. Mercury control
34. Sorbent Injection Technology
35. Electro-Catalytic Oxidation
36. K-Fuel
37. Dioxin and furan control
38. Miscellaneous associated equipment
39. Source capturing systems
40. Continuous emissions monitoring systems

Water Pollution

Water is a major constituent of every organism and thus the most important resource to man. The pollution of water makes some rivers and lake unsafe to drink or use. Water shortage could cause devastating effects on human existence.

Water pollution occurs via surface runoff, leaching to groundwater, liquid spills, wastewater discharges, eutrophication and littering. It is a large set of adverse effects upon water bodies such as lakes, rivers, oceans, and groundwater caused by human activities. Such matter deteriorates the quality of the water and renders it unfit for its intended uses. Contaminants may include organic and inorganic substances. Some organic water pollutants are:

1. Insecticides and herbicides, a huge range of organohalide and other chemicals.
2. Bacteria, often is from sewage or livestock operations.
3. Food processing waste, including pathogens.
4. Tree and brush debris from logging operations.
5. Volatile organic compounds such as industrial solvents, from improper storage.

Some inorganic water pollutants include:

1. Heavy metals including acid mine drainage.
2. Acidity caused by industrial discharges.
3. Pre-production industrial raw resin pellets, an industrial pollutant.
4. Chemical waste as industrial byproducts.
5. Fertilizers in runoff from agriculture including nitrates and phosphates.
6. Silt in surface runoff from construction sites, logging, slash and burn practices or land clearing sites.

Causes

There are many causes for water pollution but two general categories exist - direct and indirect contaminant sources. Direct sources include effluent outfalls from factories, refineries, and waste treatment plants etc. that emit fluids of varying quality directly into urban water supplies. Indirect sources include contaminants that enter the water supply from soils/groundwater systems and from the atmosphere via rain water. Soils and ground waters contain the residue of human agricultural practices (fertilizers, pesticides, etc.) and improperly disposed of industrial wastes. Atmospheric contaminants are also derived from human practices (such as gaseous emissions from automobiles, factories and even bakeries).

Thermal pollution can induce fish kills and invasion by new thermophilic species. Soil contamination is the presence of man-made chemicals or other alteration in the natural soil environment. This type of contamination typically arises from the rupture of underground storage tanks, application of pesticides, and percolation of contaminated surface water to subsurface strata, leaching of wastes from landfills or direct discharge of industrial wastes to the soil. The most common chemicals involved are petroleum hydrocarbons, solvents, pesticides, lead and other heavy metals. This occurrence of this phenomenon is correlated with the degree of industrialization and intensity of chemical usage.

Health Impacts of Water Pollution

It is a well-known fact that clean water is absolutely essential for healthy living. Adequate supply of fresh and clean drinking water is a basic need for all human beings on the earth, yet it has been observed that millions of people worldwide are deprived of this. Freshwater resources all over the world are threatened not only by over exploitation and poor management but also by ecological degradation. The main source of freshwater pollution can be attributed to discharge of untreated waste, dumping of industrial effluent, and run-off from agricultural fields. Industrial growth, urbanization and the increasing use of synthetic organic substances have serious and adverse impacts on freshwater bodies. It is a generally accepted fact that the developed countries suffer from problems of chemical discharge into the water sources mainly groundwater, while developing countries face problems of agricultural run-off in water sources. Polluted water like chemicals in drinking water causes problem to health and leads to water-borne diseases which can be prevented by taking measures that can be taken even at the household level.

Groundwater and its Contamination

Many areas of groundwater and surface water are now contaminated with heavy metals, persistent organic pollutants, and nutrients that have an adverse affect on health. Water-borne diseases and water-caused health problems are mostly due to inadequate and incompetent management of water resources. Safe water for all can only be assured when access, sustainability, and equity can be guaranteed. Access can be defined as the number of people who are guaranteed safe drinking water and sufficient quantities of it. There has to be an effort to sustain it, and there has to be a fair and equal distribution of water to all segments of the society. Urban areas generally have a higher coverage of safe water than the rural areas. Even within an area there is variation: areas that can pay for the services have access to safe water whereas areas that cannot pay for the services have to make do with water from hand pumps and other sources.

In urban areas water gets contaminated in many different ways, some of the most common reasons being leaky water pipe joints in areas where the water pipe and sewage line pass close together. Sometimes the water gets polluted at source due to various reasons and mainly due to inflow of sewage into the source. Groundwater can be contaminated through various sources and some of these are mentioned below :

1. Pesticides: Run-off from farms, backyards, and golf courses contain pesticides such as DDT that in turn contaminate the water. Leechate from landfill sites is another major contaminating source. Its effect on the ecosystems and health are endocrine and reproductive damage in wildlife. Ground-water is susceptible to contamination, as pesticides are mobile in the soil. It is a matter of concern as these chemicals are persistent in the soil and water.

2. Sewage: Untreated or inadequately treated municipal sewage is a major source of groundwater and surface water pollution in the developing countries. The organic material that is discharged with municipal waste into the watercourses uses substantial oxygen for biological degradation thereby upsetting the ecological balance of rivers and lakes. Sewage also carries microbial pathogens that are the cause of the spread of disease.

3. Nutrients: Domestic waste water, agricultural run-off, and industrial effluents contain phosphorus and nitrogen, fertilizer run-off, manure from livestock operations, which increase the level of nutrients in water bodies and can cause eutrophication in the lakes and rivers and continue on to the coastal areas. The

nitrates come mainly from the fertilizer that is added to the fields. Excessive use of fertilizers causes nitrate contamination of ground water, with the result that nitrate levels in drinking water is far above the safety levels recommended. Good agricultural practices can help in reducing the amount of nitrates in the soil and thereby lower its content in the water.

4. Synthetic organics: Many of the 1,00,000 synthetic compounds in use today are found in the aquatic environment and accumulate in the food chain. Persistent organic pollutants represent the most harmful element for the ecosystem and for human health, for example, industrial chemicals and agricultural pesticides. These chemicals can accumulate in fish and cause serious damage to human health. Where pesticides are used on a large-scale, groundwater gets contaminated and this leads to the chemical contamination of drinking water.

5. Acidification: Acidification of surface water, mainly lakes and reservoirs, is one of the major environmental impacts of transport over long distance of air pollutants such as sulphur dioxide from power plants, other heavy industry such as steel plants, and motor vehicles. This problem is more severe in the US and in parts of Europe.

Chemicals in Drinking Water

Chemicals in water can be both naturally occurring or introduced by human interference and can have serious health effects.

1. Fluoride: Fluoride in the water is essential for protection against dental caries and weakening of the bones, but higher levels can have an adverse effect on health. In India, high fluoride content is found naturally in the waters in Rajasthan.

2. Arsenic: Arsenic occurs naturally or is possibly aggravated by over powering aquifers and by phosphorus from fertilizers. High concentrations of arsenic in water can have an adverse effect on health. A few years back, high concentrations of this

element was found in drinking water at six districts in West Bengal. A majority of people in the area was found suffering from arsenic skin lesions. It was felt that arsenic contamination in the groundwater was due to natural causes. The government is trying to provide an alternative drinking water source and a method through which the arsenic content from water can be removed.

3. Lead: Pipes, fittings, solder, and the service connections of some household plumbing systems contain lead that contaminates the drinking water source.

4. Recreational use of water: Untreated sewage, industrial effluents, and agricultural waste are often discharged into the water bodies such as the lakes, coastal areas and rivers endangering their use for recreational purposes such as swimming and canoeing.

5. Petrochemicals: Petrochemicals contaminate the ground water from underground petroleum storage tanks.

6. Other heavy metals: These contaminants come from mining waste and tailings, landfills, or hazardous waste dumps.

7. Chlorinated solvents: Metal and plastic effluents, fabric cleaning, electronic and aircraft manufacturing are often discharged and contaminate groundwater.

Diseases

Water-borne diseases are infectious diseases spread primarily through contaminated water. Though these diseases are spread either directly or through flies or filth, water is the chief medium for spread of these diseases and hence they are termed as water-borne diseases.

Most intestinal (enteric) diseases are infectious and are transmitted through faecal waste. Pathogens – which include virus, bacteria, protozoa, and parasitic worms are disease-producing agents found in the faeces of infected persons. These diseases are more prevalent in areas with poor sanitary conditions. These pathogens travel through water sources and interfuses directly through persons handling food and water. Since these diseases are highly infectious, extreme care and hygiene should be maintained by people looking after an infected patient. Hepatitis, cholera, dysentery, and typhoid are the more common water-borne diseases that affect large populations in the tropical regions.

A large number of chemicals either exist naturally in the land or are added due to human activity dissolve in the water, thereby contaminating it and contributing to various diseases.

1. Pesticides: The organophosphates and the carbonates present in pesticides affect and damage the nervous system and can cause cancer. Some of the pesticides contain carcinogens that exceed recommended levels. They contain chlorides that cause reproductive and endocrinal damage.

2. Lead: Lead is hazardous to health as it accumulates in the body and affects the central nervous system. Children and pregnant women are most at risk.

3. Fluoride: Excess fluorides can cause yellowing of the teeth and damage to the spinal cord and other crippling diseases.

4. Nitrates: Drinking water that gets contaminated with nitrates can prove fatal especially to infants that drink formula milk as it restricts the amount of oxygen that reaches the brain causing the 'blue baby' syndrome. It is also linked to digestive tract cancers. It causes algae to bloom resulting in eutrophication in surface water.

5. Petrochemicals: Benzene and other petrochemicals can cause cancer even at low exposure levels.

6. Chlorinated solvents: These are linked to reproduction disorders and to some cancers.

7. Arsenic: Arsenic poisoning through water can cause liver and nervous system damage, vascular diseases and also skin cancer.

8. Other heavy metals: Heavy metals cause damage to the nervous system and the kidney, and other metabolic disruptions.

9. Salts: It makes the fresh water unusable for drinking and irrigation purposes.

Exposure to polluted water can cause diarrhoea, skin irritation, respiratory problems, and other diseases, depending on the pollutant that is in the water body. Stagnant water and other untreated water provide a habitat for the mosquito and a host of other parasites and insects that cause a large number of diseases especially in the tropical regions. Among these, malaria is undoubtedly the most widely distributed and causes most damage to human health.

Preventive Measures

Water-borne epidemics and health hazards in the aquatic environment are mainly due to improper management of water resources. Proper management of water resources has become the need of the hour as this would ultimately lead to a cleaner and healthier environment. In order to prevent the spread of water-borne infectious diseases, people should take adequate precautions. The city water supply should be properly checked and necessary steps taken to disinfect it. Water pipes should be regularly checked for leaks and cracks. At home, the water should be boiled, filtered, or other methods and necessary steps taken to ensure that it is free from infection.

Soil Pollution

Soil pollution is defined as the build-up in soils of persistent toxic compounds, chemicals, salts, radioactive materials, or disease causing agents, which have adverse effects on plant growth and animal health. Soil contamination is the presence of man-made chemicals or other alteration in the natural soil environment. This type of contamination typically arises from the rupture of underground storage tanks, application of pesticides, and percolation of contaminated surface water to subsurface strata, leaching of wastes from landfills or direct discharge of industrial wastes to the soil. The most common chemicals involved are petroleum hydrocarbons, solvents, pesticides, lead and other heavy metals. The occurrence of this phenomenon is correlated with the degree of industrialization and intensity of chemical usage.

To understand the fundamental nature of soil contamination, it is necessary to envision the variety of mechanisms for pollutants to become entrained in soil. Soil particulates may be composed of a gamut of organic and inorganic chemicals with variations in cation exchange capacity, buffering capacity, and redox potential. Most soils are mixtures of soil subtypes and thus have quite complex characteristics. There is also a great diversity of soil porosity, ranging from gravels to sands to silt to clay, pore size. Finally, there is a wide spectrum of chemical bonding or adhesion characteristics; each contaminant has a different interaction or bonding mechanism with a given soil type. On balance, some contaminants may literally drain through soils such as sand and gravel and move to other soils or deeper aquifers, while polar or organic chemicals discharged into a clay soil will have a very high adsorption. Thus most soil contamination is the result of pollutants adhering to the soil particle surface, or lodging in interstices of a soil matrix. Clearly, the equilibrium reached is a dynamic one, where new pollutants may lodge on new soil particles and the action of groundwater movement may overtime transport some of the soil contaminants to other locations or depths.

Soil contamination results when hazardous substances are either spilled or buried directly in the soil or migrate to the soil from a spill that has occurred elsewhere. For example, soil can become contaminated when small particles containing hazardous substances are released from a smokestack and are deposited on the surrounding soil as they fall out of the air.

Another source of soil contamination could be water that washes contamination from an area containing hazardous substances and deposits the contamination in the soil as it flows over or through it.

Health Effects

The major concern is that there are many sensitive land-uses where people are in direct contact with soils such as residences, parks, schools and playgrounds. Other contact mechanisms include contamination of drinking water or inhalation of soil contaminants which have vaporized. There is a very large set of health consequences from exposure to soil contamination depending on pollutant type, pathway of attack and vulnerability of the exposed population. Chromium and many of the pesticide and herbicide formulations are carcinogenic to all populations. Lead is especially hazardous to young children, in which group there is a high risk of developmental damage to the brain and nervous system, while to all populations kidney damage is a risk. Chronic exposure to benzene at sufficient concentrations is known to be associated with higher incidence of leukemia. Mercury and cyclodienes are known to induce higher incidences of kidney damage, some irreversible. PCBs and cyclodienes are linked to liver toxicity. Organophosphates and carbamates can induce a chain of responses leading to neuromuscular blockage. Many chlorinated solvents induce liver changes, kidney changes and depression of the central nervous system. There is an entire spectrum of further health effects such as headache, nausea, fatigue, eye irritation and skin rash for the above cited and other chemicals. At sufficient dosages a large number of soil contaminants cause death.

Ecosystem Effects

Not unexpectedly, soil contaminants can have significant deleterious consequences for ecosystems. There are radical soil chemistry changes which can arise from the presence of many hazardous chemicals even at low concentration of the contaminant species. These changes can manifest in the alteration of metabolism of endemic microorganisms and arthropods resident in a given soil environment. The result can be virtual eradication of some of the primary food chain, which in turn have major consequences for predator or consumer species. Even if the chemical effect on lower life forms is small, the lower pyramid levels of the food chain may ingest alien chemicals, which normally become more concentrated for each consuming rung of the food chain. Many of these effects are now well known, such as the concentration of persistent DDT materials for avian consumers, leading to weakening of egg shells, increased chick mortality and potentially species extinction.

Effects occur to agricultural lands which have certain types of soil contamination. Contaminants typically alter plant metabolism, most commonly to reduce crop yields. This has a secondary effect upon soil conservation, since the languishing crops cannot shield the earth's soil mantle from erosion phenomena. Some of these chemical contaminants have long half-lives and in other cases derivative chemicals are formed from decay of primary soil contaminants.

Control

Soil pollution has been slightly controlled by putting regulations on the use of DDT and introduction of alternatives to it. However the task of eliminating completely soil pollution is not easy, third some third world countries still utilize pollutants such as DDT as pesticides. Mining cannot be stopped because we are in constant need for mineral ores for different applications.

Cleanup Options

Cleanup or remediation is analyzed by environmental scientists who utilize field measurement of soil chemicals and also apply computer models for analyzing transport and fate of soil chemicals. There are several principal strategies for remediation:

1. Excavate soil and remove it to a disposal site away from ready pathways for human or sensitive ecosystem contact. This technique also applies to dredging of bay muds containing toxins.

2. Aeration of soils at the contaminated site.

3. Bioremediation, involving microbial digestion of certain organic chemicals. Techniques used in bioremediation include land farming, biostimulation and bioaugmentation soil biota with commercially available microflora.

4. Extraction of groundwater or soil vapor with an active electromechanical system, with subsequent stripping of the contaminants from the extract.

5. Containment of the soil contaminants (such as by capping or paving over in place).

Noise Pollution

Noise pollution is displeasing human or machine created sound that disrupts the activity or happiness of human or animal life. A common form of noise pollution is from transportation, principally motor vehicles.

Sources of Noise

The source of most noise worldwide is transportation systems, principally motor vehicle noise, but also including aircraft noise and rail noise. Poor urban planning may give rise to noise pollution, since side-by-side industrial and residential buildings can results in noise pollution in the residential area. Other sources are office equipment, factory machinery, construction work, appliances, power tools, lighting hum and audio entertainment systems. Noise from recreational vehicles has become a problem.

Human Health

Noise health effects are both health and behavioral in nature. The unwanted sound is called noise pollution. This unwanted sound can damage physiological and psychological health. Noise pollution can cause annoyance and aggression, hypertension, high stress levels, tinnitus, hearing loss, and other harmful effects. Furthermore, stress and hypertension are the leading causes to health problems, whereas tinnitus can lead to forgetfulness, severe depression and at times panic attacks. The mechanism for chronic exposure to noise leading to hearing loss is well established. The elevated sound levels cause trauma to the cochlear structure in the inner ear, which gives rise to irreversible hearing loss. A very loud sound in a particular frequency range can damage the cochlea's hair cells that respond to that range thereby reducing the ear's ability to hear those frequencies in the future. However, loud noise in any frequency range has deleterious effects across the entire range of human hearing. The outer ear (visible portion of the human ear) combined with the middle ear amplifies sound levels by a factor of 20 when sound reaches the inner ear. High noise levels can contribute to cardiovascular effects and exposure to moderately high levels during a single eight hour period causes a statistical rise in blood pressure of five to ten points and an increase in stress and vasoconstriction leading to the increased blood pressure noted above as well as to increased incidence of coronary artery disease.

Noise can have a detrimental effect on animals by causing stress, increasing risk of mortality by changing the delicate balance in predator/prey detection and avoidance, and by interfering with their use of sounds in communication especially in relation to reproduction and in navigation. Acoustic overexposure can lead to temporary or permanent loss of hearing. An impact of noise on animal life is the reduction of usable habitat that noisy areas may cause, which in the case of endangered species may be part of the path to extinction. One of the best known cases of damage caused by noise pollution is the death of certain species of beached whales, brought on by the extremely loud (up to 200 decibels) sound of military sonar.

Mitigation and Control of Noise

There are a variety of strategies for mitigating roadway noise including use of noise barriers, limitation of vehicle speeds, alteration of roadway surface texture, limitation of heavy duty vehicles, use of traffic controls that smooth vehicle flow to reduce braking and acceleration and tire design. An important factor in applying these strategies is a computer model for roadway noise that is capable of addressing local topography, meteorology, traffic operations and hypothetical mitigation. Costs of building-in mitigation can be modest, provided these solutions are sought in the planning stage of a roadway project. Aircraft noise can be reduced to some extent by design of quieter jet engines.

Solid Waste Management

Solid waste management includes all activities that seek to minimize the health, environmental and aesthetic impacts of solid wastes. Solid waste can be defined as material that no longer has any value to the person who is responsible for it, and is not intended to be discharged through a pipe. It does not normally include human excreta. It is generated by domestic, commercial, industrial, healthcare, agricultural and mineral extraction activities and accumulates in streets and public places. The words "garbage", "trash", "refuse" and "rubbish" are used to refer to some forms of solid waste.

Solid wastes are generated by many different activities. Very large quantities are produced by agriculture and mining, but these wastes will not be considered in this introduction. Wastes from houses, streets, shops, offices, industries and hospitals are usually the responsibility of municipal or other governmental authorities, and it is these wastes which are the subject of this article. The preparation and management of a good solid waste management system needs inputs from a range of disciplines, and careful consideration of local conditions. If solid wastes are not managed properly, there are many negative impacts that may result. Some of the most important are mentioned in the following list. The relative importance of each depends very much on local conditions.

1. Uncollected wastes often end up in drains, causing blockages which result in flooding and unsanitary conditions.

2. Flies breed in some constituents of solid wastes, and flies are very effective vectors that spread disease.

3. Mosquitoes breed in blocked drains and in rainwater that is retained in discarded cans, tyres and other objects. Mosquitoes spread disease, including malaria and dengue.

4. Rats find shelter and food in waste dumps. Rats consume and spoil food, spread disease, damage electrical cables and other materials and inflict unpleasant bites.

5. The open burning of waste causes air pollution; the products of combustion include dioxins which are particularly hazardous.

6. Aerosols and dusts can spread fungi and pathogens from uncollected and decomposing wastes.

7. Uncollected waste degrades the urban environment, discouraging efforts to keep streets and open spaces in a clean and attractive condition. Solid waste management is a clear indicator of the effectiveness of a municipal administration - if

the provision of this service is inadequate large numbers of citizens are aware of it.

8. Plastic bags are a particular aesthetic nuisance and they cause the death of grazing animals which eat them.

9. Waste collection workers face particular occupational hazards, including strains from lifting, injuries from sharp objects and traffic accidents.

10. Dumps of waste and abandoned vehicles block streets and other access ways.

11. Dangerous items (such as broken glass, razor blades, hypodermic needles and other healthcare wastes, aerosol cans and potentially explosive containers and chemicals from industries) may pose risks of injury or poisoning, particularly to children and people who sort through the waste.

12. Heavy refuse collection trucks can cause significant damage to the surfaces of roads that were not designed for such weights.

13. Waste items that are recycled without being cleaned effectively or sterilized can transmit infection to later users. (Examples are bottles and medical supplies.)

14. Polluted water (leachate) flowing from waste dumps and disposal sites can cause serious pollution of water supplies. Chemical wastes (especially persistent organics) may be fatal or have serious effects if ingested, inhaled or touched and can cause widespread pollution of water supplies.

15. Large quantities of waste that have not been placed according to good engineering practice can slip and collapse, burying and killing people.

16. Waste that is treated or disposed of in unsatisfactory ways can cause a severe aesthetic nuisance in terms of smell and appearance.

17. Liquids and fumes, escaping from deposits of chemical wastes (perhaps formed as a result of chemical reactions between components in the wastes), can have fatal or other serious effects.

18. Landfill gas (which is produced by the decomposition of wastes) can be explosive if it is allowed to accumulate in confined spaces (such as the cellars of buildings).

19. Methane (one of the main components of landfill gas) is much more effective than carbon dioxide as a greenhouse gas, leading to climate change.

20. Fires on disposal sites can cause major air pollution, causing illness and reducing visibility, making disposal sites dangerously unstable, causing explosions of cans, and possibly spreading to adjacent property.

21. Former disposal sites provide very poor foundation support for large buildings, so buildings constructed on former sites are prone to collapse.

Resource Recovery

Resource recovery means the obtaining of some economic benefit from material that someone has regarded as waste. It includes reuse - being used for the same purpose again (such as refilling a soft drinks bottle); recovery - processing material so that it can be used again as the same material, such as the processing of waste paper to make pulp and then new paper; conversion - processing the material to make something different (such as producing padding for clothing and sleeping bags from plastic bottles, or producing compost from food waste); energy recovery - usually referring to the burning of waste so that the heat can be used (for example, for heating swimming pools). Another method of energy recovery is to collect the gas that is produced in very large sanitary landfills and use it as a fuel or to generate electricity.

Some key factors that affect the potential for resource recovery are the cost of the separated material, its purity, its quantity and its location. The costs of storage and transport are major factors that decide the economic potential for resource recovery. In many low-income countries, the fraction of material that is won for resource recovery is very high, because this work is done in a very labour-intensive way, and for very low incomes. In such situations the creation of employment is the main economic benefit of resource recovery. The situation in industrialized countries is very different, since resource recovery is undertaken by the formal sector, driven by law and a general public concern for the environment, and often at considerable expense.

Composting is an excellent method of recycling bio-degradable waste from an ecological point of view. However, many large and small composting schemes have failed because composting is regarded as a disposal process, and not a production process. It is essential to pay careful attention to the marketing and the quality of the product. Composting should be an activity of the agricultural sector, not the waste management sector.

Disposal

It appears that in most low-income countries, and many medium income countries, very little progress has been made in upgrading waste disposal operations. Open dumps, where the waste is unloaded in piles, make very uneconomical use of the available space, allow free access to waste pickers, animals and flies and often produce unpleasant and hazardous smoke from slow-burning fires.

A sanitary landfill is a site where solid wastes are placed on or in the ground at a carefully selected location by means of engineering techniques that minimize pollution of air, water and soil, and other risks to man and animals. Aesthetic considerations are also taken into account.

In some major cities loans or grants have been used to construct sanitary landfills on sites that have been carefully chosen, but usually little attention is paid to the training of a site manager and to the provision of sufficient financial and physical resources to allow a reasonable standard of operation. As a result, some sites quickly degenerate into open dumps. It is crucial to good operations to have a motivated and trained site manager. It is recommended that the training for this position should include practical experience on well-run sites.

Most sanitary landfill designs attach considerable importance to preventing polluted water (leachate) escaping from the site. It has been shown that large quantities of leachate can be produced by landfills, even in semi-arid climates. Most designs include expensive and carefully constructed impermeable layers which prevent leachate moving downwards into the ground and drainage systems to bring the leachate to a treatment plant or a storage tank. However, if the tank is not emptied before it overflows, or if the plant is not working, the leachate control system actually makes the pollution worse than from an open dump, because all the leachate is concentrated in one place, giving natural purification systems very little chance of reducing the pollution impact. This example shows that good design and construction can achieve nothing if they are not followed by good operation.

Healthcare wastes are generated as a result of activities related to the practice of medicine (including veterinary medicine and dentistry). Often this term is used to refer only to solid wastes. Some of the healthcare wastes coming from any particular hospital or institution are similar in nature to domestic solid wastes, and may be called "general healthcare wastes". The remaining wastes pose serious health hazards because of their physical, chemical or biological nature, and so are known as "hazardous healthcare wastes" or "healthcare risk wastes". Wastes which are particularly offensive because of their appearance or smell may also be classed with the hazardous wastes.

Healthcare wastes have attracted considerable attention because of the emotional impact of seeing body parts amidst solid waste, and because of the increasing concern about AIDS and hepatitis. In many cases the most dangerous items in healthcare wastes are needles from syringes and drips, because the needles shield the viruses from chemical disinfectants and a harsh external environment, and the sharp point allows easy access for the viruses into the blood stream of anyone who is pricked by the needle.

Many attempts to upgrade healthcare waste management rely solely on the provision of incinerators or other treatment technologies. Such a strategy has several weaknesses in that often the hospitals and healthcare facilities are not able to afford the operating costs of the plant, and so the plants are left unused or not repaired when the break down; many of the risks occur before the waste gets to this final stage, and so they are not reduced by the provision of treatment equipment; the real need often provides better methods of storage to train the staff to adopt safer working practices.

Some waste materials need special care because their properties make them more hazardous or problematic than general wastes. Used oil can be refined for reuse or burned in properly equipped furnaces. Slaughterhouse wastes should be buried in special trenches at suitable sites. Car tyres should be reused as much as possible, and carefully protected from open burning. Chemical wastes from some industries (including tanning, dry-cleaning, photographic processing and many chemical production industries) and unwanted pesticides and other agricultural chemicals, should be collected under close supervision and treated in appropriate ways. The management of hazardous chemicals is not only a matter of technology and legislation, but also of enforcement, funding and financial instruments. Some wastes are so hazardous and expensive to treat that priority attention should be focused on changing to processes them so, use substitutes that are less hazardous, and to minimizing the quantities that are discarded. Indeed, minimization and substitution should be seen as the preferred options in dealing with any difficult waste.

Waste Management Methods

Waste management is the collection, transport, processing, recycling or disposal of waste materials. The term usually relates to materials produced by human activity, and is generally undertaken to reduce their effect on health, aesthetics or amenity. Waste management is also carried out to reduce the materials' effect on the environment and to recover resources from them. Waste management can involve solid, liquid or gaseous substances, with different methods and fields of expertise for each.

Waste management practices differ for developed and developing nations, for urban and rural areas, and for residential and industrial, producers. Management for non-hazardous residential and institutional waste in metropolitan areas is usually the responsibility of local government authorities, while management for non-hazardous commercial and industrial waste is usually the responsibility of the generator. Waste management methods vary widely between areas for many reasons, including type of waste material, nearby land uses, and the area available.

Disposal

1. Landfill

Disposing of waste in a landfill involves burying waste to dispose of it, and this remains a common practice in most countries. Historically, landfills were often established in disused quarries, mining voids or borrow pits. A properly-designed and well-managed landfill can be a hygienic and relatively inexpensive method of disposing of waste materials. Older, poorly-designed or poorly-managed landfills can create a number of adverse environmental impacts such as wind-blown litter, attraction of vermin, and generation of liquid leachate. Another common byproduct of landfills is gas (mostly composed of methane and carbon dioxide), which is produced as organic waste breaks down anaerobically. This gas can create odor problems, kill surface vegetation, and is a greenhouse gas.

Design characteristics of a modern landfill include methods to contain leachate such as clay or plastic lining material. Deposited waste is normally compacted to increase its density and stability, and covered to prevent attracting vermin (such as mice or rats). Many landfills also have landfill gas extraction systems installed to extract the landfill gas. Gas is pumped out of the landfill using perforated pipes and flared off or burnt in a gas engine to generate electricity.

Many local authorities, especially in rural areas, have found it difficult to establish new landfills due to opposition from owners of adjacent land. As a result, solid waste disposal in these areas must be transported further for disposal or managed by other methods. This fact, as well as growing concern about the environmental impacts of excessive materials consumption, has given rise to efforts to minimize the amount of waste sent to landfill in many areas. These efforts include taxing or levying waste sent to landfill, recycling waste products, converting waste to energy, and designing products that use less material.

2. Incineration

Incineration is a disposal method that involves combustion of waste material. Incineration and other high temperature waste treatment systems are sometimes described as "thermal treatment". Incinerators convert waste materials into heat, gas, steam and ash.

Incineration is carried out both on a small scale by individuals, and on a large scale by industry. It is used to dispose of solid, liquid and gaseous waste. It is recognised as a practical method of disposing of certain hazardous waste materials (such as biological medical waste). Although it remains a controversial method of waste disposal in many places due to issues such as emission of gaseous pollutants, modern combustion technologies such as the RCBC (rotary cascading bed combustor) allow efficient energy production with emissions well within regulatory standards.

Incineration is common in countries such as Japan where land is more scarce, as these facilities generally do not require as much area as landfills. Waste-to-energy (WtE) or energy-from-waste (EfW) are broad terms for incinerator facilities that burn waste in a furnace or boiler to generate heat, steam and/or electricity.

Recycling

The definition of recycling is to pass a substance through a system that enables that substance to be reused. Waste recycling involves the collection of waste materials and the separation and clean-up of those materials. Recycling waste means that fewer new products and consumables need to be produced, saving raw materials and reducing energy consumption. There are a number of different methods by which waste material is recycled: the raw materials may be extracted and reprocessed, or the calorific content of the waste may be converted to electricity. New methods of recycling are being developed continuously, and are described briefly below :

Physical reprocessing

The popular meaning of 'recycling' in most developed countries refers to the widespread collection and reuse of everyday waste materials such as empty beverage containers.

These are collected and sorted into common types so that the raw materials from which the items are made can be reprocessed into new products. Material for recycling may be collected separately from general waste using dedicated bins and collection vehicles, or sorted directly from mixed waste streams.

The most common consumer products recycled include aluminium beverage cans, steel food and aerosol cans, HDPE and PET bottles, glass bottles and jars, paperboard cartons, newspapers, magazines, and cardboard. Other types of plastic (PVC, LDPE, PP and PS: see resin identification code) are also recyclable, although these are not as commonly collected. These items are usually composed of a single type of material, making them relatively easy to recycle into new products. The recycling of complex products (such as computers and electronic equipment) is more difficult, due to the additional dismantling and separation required.

Biological processing

Waste materials that are organic in nature, such as plant material, food scraps, and paper products, can be recycled using biological composting and digestion processes to decompose the organic matter. The resulting organic material is then recycled as mulch or compost for agricultural or landscaping purposes. In addition, waste gas from the process (such as methane) can be captured and used for generating electricity. The intention of biological processing in waste management is to control and accelerate the natural process of decomposition of organic matter.

There is a large variety of composting and digestion methods and technologies varying in complexity from simple home compost heaps, to industrial-scale enclosed-vessel digestion of mixed domestic waste (see Mechanical biological treatment). Methods of biological decomposition are differentiated as being aerobic or anaerobic methods, though hybrids of the two methods also exist.

Energy recovery

The energy content of waste products can be harnessed directly by using them as a direct combustion fuel, or indirectly by processing them into another type of fuel. Recycling through thermal treatment ranges from using waste as a fuel source for cooking or heating to fuel for boilers to generate steam and electricity in a turbine. Pyrolysis and gasification are two related forms of thermal treatment where waste materials are heated to high temperatures with limited oxygen availability. The process typically occurs in a sealed vessel under high pressure. Pyrolysis of solid waste converts the material into solid, liquid and gas products. The liquid and gas can be burnt to produce energy or refined into other products. The solid residue (char) can be further refined into products such as activated carbon. Gasification is used to convert organic materials directly into a synthetic gas (syngas) composed of carbon monoxide and hydrogen. The gas is then burnt to produce electricity and steam.

Avoidance and reduction

Another important method of waste management is the prevention of waste material being created. Methods of avoidance include reuse of second-hand products, repairing broken items instead of buying new, designing products to be refillable or reusable (such as cotton instead of plastic shopping bags), encouraging consumers to avoid using disposable products (such as disposable cutlery), and designing products that use less material to achieve the same purpose.

Waste Management Concepts

There are a number of concepts about waste management which vary in their usage between countries or regions. This section presents some of the most general, widely-used concepts.

Waste hierarchy

1. The waste hierarchy

The waste hierarchy refers to the "3 R's" reduce, reuse and recycle, which classify waste management strategies according to their desirability in terms of waste minimization. The waste hierarchy remains the cornerstone of most waste minimization strategies. The aim of the waste hierarchy is to extract the maximum practical benefits from products and to generate the minimum amount of waste.

2. Extended producer responsibility

Extended Producer Responsibility (EPR) is a strategy designed to promote the integration of all costs associated with products throughout their life cycle (including end-of-life disposal costs) into the market price of the product. Extended producer responsibility is meant to impose accountability over the entire life cycle of products and packaging introduced to the market. This means that firms which manufacture, import and/or sell products are required to be responsible for the products after their useful life as well as during manufacture.

3. Polluter pays principle

The Polluter Pays Principle is a principle where the polluting party pays for the impact caused to the natural environment. With respect to waste management, this generally refers to the requirement for a waste generator to pay for appropriate disposal of the waste. Due to the implementation of modern solid waste management practices, both the public health and the quality of the environment are benefited directly and substantially.

A modern solid waste management program can be implemented for a reasonable cost. This is an important fact because there are ample known situations where solid waste management costs in developing countries are high and the level of service low. But, if the underlying reasons for these situations are analysed, then one can see in many cases that cost-effective waste management systems would result if the identified deficiencies in the systems were remedied.

For example, in some developing countries, municipalities spend a disproportionate amount of financial resources on certain solid waste services, in particular waste collection and sweeping. Unfortunately, high capital investment in the solid waste management sector in many developing countries does not necessarily lead to improvements in the quality of service. On the other hand, substantial improvements can be achieved in many cases by making low-cost, or sometimes no-cost, modifications in the existing system, with the focus being on increasing system efficiencies. Examples of such improvements are the efficient design of collection routes, modifications in the collection vehicles, reductions in equipment downtime, and public education, (e.g., education and communication leading to the production of less waste and the reduction of litter).

Recovery and Utilization of Resources

For several reasons, resource recovery is a major element in solid waste management in developing nations. Reclaimable inorganic components (metals, glass, plastic, textiles and others) traditionally have been recovered mostly by way of unregulated manual scavenging by private individuals (typically known as the "informal" sector). In recent years, the trend is to formalize and mechanize scavenging through the establishment of material recovery facilities (MRFs). Reuse and recovery of the inorganic components of the waste stream is an important aspect of waste management.

Special attention is given to organic (biodegradable) residues since, in the majority of developing countries, these residues constitute at least 50% of the waste (by weight). The resource recovery aspect regarding the organic component is threefold:

1. The component can be used in agriculture as a soil amendment through composting.

2. Its energy content can be recovered either biologically or thermally. Biological energy recovery is by way of methane production through anaerobic digestion. Thermal recovery is by way of combustion to produce heat.

3. The organic content can be hydrolyzed either chemically or enzymatically to produce a sugar. The sugar can be used as a substrate for ethanol fermentation or for single-cell protein production.

Of the three applications, use in agriculture is the most practical. Although dating back many years, methane production ("biogasification") has only recently begun to receive serious attention as a potential alternative source of energy. Many hurdles, primarily economic in nature, must be surmounted before either single-celled protein production or ethanol fermentation become a practical reality. Last but not least, the availability, size, and continuity of a market or some form of demand for the reclaimed resource must be determined, lest recycling become merely a prelude to land filling.

8

BIOTERRORISM

Terrorism is a voluntary action to terrorize innocent people by violence especially for political purpose. Bioterrorism or biological warfare has been defined as the employment of biological agents to produce casualties in man or animals or damage to plants. It has also been defined as the deliberate release of disease causing germs with the intent of killing large numbers of people and of panicking many more. Biological warfare is practically using germs (micro-organisms) or toxins produced by them as weapons of mass destruction of people. Genetically modified micro-organisms are also used to cause treatment resistant infection and destruction to crops and livestock necessary for human survival. Biological weapons are a real threat to the public health of any country in the world and none appears prepared.

Biological Agents

Biological agents include micro-organisms and toxins produced by them. Chemicals obtained from plant materials are also used as biological agents to create bioterrorism. Micro-organisms used for bioterrorism are bacteria, rickettsia, viruses and bacterial toxins. The agents are used in the form of ultra fine powder or as an aerosol. They are either released into the environment or mixed in water or food. Incubation period varies with each biological agent. Further, duration of illness, symptoms, means of transmission and treatment also differ to a great extent. Toxins used for bioterrorism are toxic chemical compounds synthesized in nature by living organism especially by micro-organisms. Classifiable by molecular weight, source, preferred targets in the body and mechanism of action, they include the most potent poisons on the planet but there are practical limits on their use as bioagents for bioterrorism. Botulinum toxin produced by a bacterium and ricin produced by castor seed are the most important toxin threats on the battle field or in bio-warfare. Some of the potential biological agents which are most promising in bio-warfare have been described below.

Anthrax

Anthrax is a naturally occurring disease of plant eating animals, particularly cattle and sheep. This disease has been around here on the planet for tens of thousands of years. The germ is a gram-positive bacterium called *Bacillus anthracis* that seeds itself by forming long lasting spores. It produces two virulence factors, the anthrax toxin and an anti-phagocytic polypeptide capsule. The spores of this bacterium can survive in the environment for a long time. People can catch anthrax from infected animals or contaminated animal products. Three forms of the disease occur on the basis of their mode of transmission. They are cutaneous, intestinal and inhalation anthrax. Cutaneous (skin) anthrax infection develops when a bacterial organism from infected animal tissues becomes deposited under the skin. This form of infection is acquired by butchering, skinning or dissecting infected carcass or by handling contaminated wool, hair, etc. This disease is common in workers dealing with these materials. Skin infection starts with an itchy bump like a mosquito bite. After a day or two, it forms a small liquid filled sac. This sac then becomes a painless ulcer with an area of black dead tissue in the middle. The incubation period for this infection is from one to seven days. Antibiotic treatment cures this infection. Untreated anthrax kills about one in five people.

Intestinal anthrax is frequently contracted by cattle and sheep that ingest anthrax spores by grazing on pastures or on the hay produced from pastures where anthrax infected animals have died or been buried. Such pastures may remain infectious for many years. When eaten the food or meat contaminated with anthrax spores by man, intestinal anthrax infection develops. This infection is characterized by an acute inflammation of the intestinal tract. Initial signs of nausea, loss of appetite, vomiting and fever are followed by abdominal pain, vomiting of blood and severe diarrohea. Untreated intestinal anthrax is deadly.

Inhalation anthrax is the most deadly form of the disease. It develops when the bacterial organism is inhaled into the lungs. It begins after an incubation period of 1-6 days, depending upon the dose of inhaled organisms. Onset of the infection is gradual and non-specific with fever and fatigue, sometimes in association with a non-productive cough and mild chest discomfort. The patient may briefly improve after 2-4 days but within 24 hours, after this brief improvement, respiratory distress occurs with shock and death following shortly thereafter. Penicillin antibiotic has been recommended for this infection but in case of penicillin-sensitive patients-tetracycline, erythromycin, chloramphenicol, gentamicin, and ciprofloxacin are recommended. In USA, there had not been a case of inhalation anthrax since 1978 until the recent case that happened in September 2001. Inhalation anthrax is not uncommon in southern India.

When anthrax spores get inside the body, they grow rapidly and cause infection. They produce a dangerous substance called anthrax toxin that kills cells of the immune system. This toxin is so deadly that it can kill even after infection is brought under control. All forms of anthrax if diagnosed early enough can be cured by prompt antibiotic treatment. However, some anthrax strains developed as biological weapons are resistant to many drugs.

Anthrax has been called the perfect germ for bio-terrorism. The attack is target-oriented. This is because it is not contagious which means that it does not spread from person to person. Only those exposed to a release of spores get sick. The spores last for a long time in the soil. During World War II, the British Army experimented with an explosive shell filled with anthrax spores. These experiments took place on an island off the coast of Scotland. Spores persisted in the environment for 36 years. A massive decontamination effort cleared the region in 1987. Nevertheless, it is easy to grow deadly anthrax and it is even harder to make it into a weapon. The spores have to be turned into a microscopically fine powder which is no simple trick. Then the powder must be sprayed over a large area with a specially adapted device. Even then, the temperature and wind must be exactly right to contaminate populated areas.

Botulism

It is a severe and often fatal type of food poisoning caused by potent protein neurotoxins produced by a gram-positive anaerobic bacterium, *Clostridium botulinum*. The bacterium produces seven distinct neurotoxins. A biological warfare attack with botulinum toxin delivered by aerosol would be expected to cause symptoms similar in most respects to those observed with food borne botulism. In pure form, the toxin is a white crystalline substance and dissolves readily in water. But it decays rapidly in the open air. Symptoms of inhalation botulism may begin as early as 24-36 hours following exposure or as late as several days. Initial signs and symptoms include generalized weakness, lassitude and dizziness. Diminished salivation with extreme dryness of the mouth and throat may cause complaints of a sore throat. Urinary retention may occur. Respiratory failure secondary to paralysis of respiratory muscles is the most serious complication and eventually causes death.

Clostridium perfringens is a common anaerobic bacterium associated with three distinct disease syndromes: gas gangrene, enteritis necroticans and food poisoning. Each of these syndromes has very specific requirements for delivering inocula of this bacterium to specific sites to induce disease. Gas gangrene is well recognized, life threatening emergency. This bacterium produces toxins that create high mortality and which produce the characteristic intense pain. Within hours signs of systemic toxicity appear including confusion and sweating. It produces large amounts of carbon dioxide and hydrogen that cause intense swelling which is termed as gas gangrene resulting in gas in the soft tissues and the emission of foul smelling gas from the wound. Clinical features include necrosis, dark red serous fluid and numerous gas filled vesicles. No specific treatment is available for *C. perfringens* intoxication. Early antibiotic treatment with penicillin or clindamycin or rifampin is effective. Late treatment is not effective because by then significant amounts of toxins accumulate in the body and enter the bloodstream causing fatal systemic illness. At least 12 protein toxins are elaborated and one or more of these could be produced, concentrated and used as a biological weapon like *C. botulinum*. Therefore, these two *Clostridium* species serve as potential biological weapons for use in biological warfare.

Brucellosis

Brucellosis is a disease caused by gram-negative, aerobic, non-motile bacteria, *Brucella melitensis, B. abortus* and *B. suis*. *Brucella* species are mainly parasites and pathogens of domestic animals. *B. melitensis* occurs in sheep and goats, *B. abortus* in cattle and *B. suis* in swine. Humans are infected when they inhale contaminated aerosols, ingest raw infected milk or meat with the bacteria. Generally brucellosis is an occupational disease for Veterinarians butchers and slaughter house workers. In humans, brucellosis occurs after an incubation period of 3-4 weeks. The disease is characterized by generalized aches and pains of the muscles and joints, headaches, chills and night sweats, and a prolonged, irregular fever and which continues into a chronic stage. Brucellas initially multiply within lymph nodes and later pass to the bloodstream. Here, antibodies formed by the patient act in conjunction with complement to cause bacteriolysis and liberation of endotoxin which causes the fever response and other generalized symptoms. Many of the blood borne bacteria are removed by macrophages of the liver, spleen, lymph node and bone marrow. The bacteria continue to survive and grow within the macrophages. Tetracycline is the drug of choice for treatment of brucellosis in humans. No vaccine is available for human immunization but live attenuated vaccines are available for immunization of cattle, sheep and goats. *Brucella* species have long been considered as potential candidates for use in biological warfare. Under selected environmental conditions such as darkness, cool temperature and high carbon dioxide, *Brucella* species persist for up to 2 years. When used as biological warfare agent, brucellae would most likely be delivered by the aerosol route, the resulting infection would be expected to mimic natural disease.

Plague

Plague is an acute, specific communicable disease caused by facultatively anaerobic, gram-negative bacterium, *Yersinia pestis*. It is transmitted by the bite of infected oriental rat flea, *Xenopsylla cheopsis*, or the human flea, *Pulex irritans*. Plague is primarily a disease of rodents and man is affected incidentally. First description of plague epidemic is available during the Jahangir period in Agra. Plague remains a major life threatening infection of human beings and animals. The disease took a heavy toll of life in the early part of the century with an estimated 12.5 million human deaths in the last pandemic which started in 1889 and involved widely scattered areas in the country. It is occurring in cyclic form every 3-5 years or 8-10 years. Last episodes were in 1966 in Karnataka. However, after the gap of 28 years, there was an outbreak in 1994 in Maharashtra and Gujarat.

Y. pestis appears like bipolar safety pin and produces endotoxin and exotoxin that result into fatal toxic symptoms. It is also found in rat burrows as they multiply in their favourable micro-climate. The disease is transmitted from rat to rat and human by the bite of a rat flea. The main reservoirs of infection are wild rodents like field mice, skunks and others. There are three clinical types of plague under natural conditions - bubonic, primary septicemia and pneumonic. In bubonic plague, the incubation period ranges from 2 to 10 days. It is characterised by high fever, chills, nausea, vomiting, general weakness and enlarged inflamed lymph glands (bubos). It is not infective stage. The exudates from bubos are filled with plague bacilli. The mortality rate is 50 per cent in untreated patients; this stage sometimes ends into septicemia, the incubation period of which is 2-7 days. In this stage, bacteria spreads to the central nervous system, lungs and elsewhere. The spread of bacteria to lungs is called pneumonic plague. The incubation period for this form is 1 to 3 days. It is characterised by thin watery sputum with bright red streaks of blood and it has nearly a 100 per cent mortality rate if untreated. This form of plague spreads from man to man by droplet or sputum. All ages and both sexes are susceptible. Streptomycin, tetracycline, and chloramphenicol are highly effective if treatment has begun early. Vaccination against plague is available. Since plague is highly fatal, it can be used as a biological weapon. It could be delivered via contaminated fleas causing the bubonic type or via aerosol causing the pneumonic type.

Smallpox

Smallpox has been afflicting mankind for centuries. It is an extremely serious disease and probably the most important disease. It is caused by *Variola* virus and transmitted by droplet infection, either directly from an infected person to another person or by handling of articles infected by the smallpox patient. Incubation period in the infected person is typically 12 days. The virus is believed to lodge in the naso-pharynx and to invade the regional lymphatic system. This is followed by dissemination of virus via the blood stream to all tissues and especially the skin. An initial fever occurs, followed by a rash consisting of various stages of lesions, from macules to papules to vesicles to pustules. The pustules become larger and are filled with fluid. The fever recurs and the patient becomes severely ill with generalized symptoms. The pustules finally form crusts and upon healing leave depressed de-pigmented scars on the face for life time. In treated patients, permanent joint deformities and blindness may follow recovery. Vaccine immunity may prevent or modify illness.

There are two kinds of *Variola* virus: 1) *Variola major,* which causes severe symptoms and has a fatality rate of 10-30 per cent 2) the less virulent *Variola minor,* with a fatality rate of only 0.1 to 0.3 per cent. There is no natural resistance to smallpox in the world. In 1958, the world health assembly adopted the recommendation that WHO should initiate the eradication of smallpox on a worldwide scale and the 33rd World Health Assembly declared that Worldwide eradication of smallpox was achieved starting first in South America, then in Asia and last in Africa where the last case of endemic smallpox recorded in 1977 in Somalia. The eradication of *Variola* virus causing smallpox was defined as eradication of clinical forms of smallpox not as the final eradication of the *Variola* virus. The virus exists today in only two laboratory repositories in the U.S. and Russia, in collaboration with WHO. The organisation tried many a time to destroy the virus in good intention but failed. Appearance of human cases of smallpox outside the laboratory would signal use of the virus as a biological weapon. As smallpox is a communicable disease and deadly, it is considered to be a potential biological weapon.

SARS

Corona viruses are human and animal pathogens. In humans, they cause common cold and in animals they cause the infections such as bronchitis in chickens, hepatitis in mouse and gastroenteritis in piglets. Corona viruses tend to mutate quickly and defy treatment, the common cold in humans behaves in the same way. SARS means Severe Acute Respiratory Syndrome, a deadly respiratory illness caused by a corona virus. Regarding the origin of SARS virus there are different opinions. A group of scientists in the United Kingdom asserts that the virus that causes SARS may hail from outer space. Some opine that the virus came from outer space through asteroids, leonids and meteoroids in frozen form. This virus first reached the Himalayan ranges and from there it found its way into some animals in China. Some others are of the opinion that the indigenous corona virus in animals such as wild game, endangered snakes and turtles and civet cats (native of Africa and Asia) jumped to humans. Because, there has been a close contact between these animals and humans in southern China, World Health Organization reports show that civet cats are largely responsible for SARS infection in humans. First report of SARS came from China. There, the earliest patients of SARS were in close contact with chickens, ducks, pigeons and owls. Vendors of these birds were the first patients to become ill with SARS in China's Guangdong province. The animals in which the SARS virus thrives are not affected but only humans are affected when exposed to this virus. The SARS virus thrives well in the stools and respiratory secretions of animals, especially civet cats. If any body touches the surface that is contaminated with virus and one is simply transferring the virus to his/her mucous membrane. In effect he or she is infected. Fatality depends on the health of the individual if one has some other underlying disease the fatality rate is high. The virus thrives in human waste; it is more stable in stool from diarrhoea patients than in normal stool where it could only be found for few hours. The virus thrives well under alkaline conditions which occur in the stool in diarrohea. The stool of newborns is more acidic, kills the virus after three hours. The SARS patients are classified into two groups: Super spreaders and ordinary spreaders. Super spreaders are individuals who spread the virus to larger number of people while ordinary spreaders are individuals who spread the virus to fewer than three people. The characteristic features of SARS virus indicate that it can serve as a vital biological weapon because it spreads very fast when released through stools or respiratory secretions and causes illness or death.

Ricin

Ricin is a glycoprotein toxin obtained from the seeds of the castor plant. It blocks protein synthesis by altering the genetic material RNA, thus killing the cell. Ricin's significance as a potential biological warfare agent relates to its availability worldwide, its ease of production and extreme respiratory toxicity when inhaled. Recently, there are reports of ricin vials found in places where they are not expected to be found in UK and France. As ricin is a potential biological weapon, easy to carry and use at the target places, it is given top priority for use as a biological weapon.

Clinical picture seen with ricin as the cause of illness depends on the route of exposure. All reported serious or fatal cases of castor bean ingestion have taken approximately the same course: rapid onset of nausea, vomiting, abdominal cramps and severe diarrohea with vascular collapse; death occurred on the third day or later following inhalation of ricin powder, one might expect non-specific symptoms of weakness, fever, cough, etc., followed by hypotension and cardiovascular collapse. The exact cause of death is still unknown but it is felt it, varies with the route of intoxication. High doses of inhalation appear to produce severe enough respiratory damage to cause death.

Episodes of Bioterrorism

As early biological warfare took place in the Black sea port of Kaffa, Ukraine in 1346. Rats and their fleas carried the plague disease to attacking soldiers from Tatar in the East Asian mainland. Another attempted use of biological warfare occurred between 1754 and 1767 when the British infiltrated small pox infected blankets to unsuspecting American Indians during the French and Indian War. Smallpox decimated the Indians. In 1932 the Japanese began a series of horrific experiments on human beings outside Harbin, Manchuria, China. At least 11 Chinese cities were attacked with the agents of anthrax, cholera, shigellosis, salmonella and plague and at least 10,000 people died during their gruesome experiments. Yellow rain caused by *Trichothecene mycotoxins*, attacks in south-east Asia caused thousands of deaths between 1974 and 1981. In 1978, Bulgarian dissident George Markov was assassinated using an Umbrella Gun that shot ricin into his thigh. In 1979 about 66 people died of inhalation anthrax when an aerosol of *Bacillus anthracis* spores was accidentally released from a biological warfare research facility in USSR. By 1991, the Iraqis had weaponized anthrax, botulinum toxin and aflatoxin. The United Nations destroyed the Iraq's offensive biological warfare facilities in 1996. In 1995, sarin nerve gas was released in a Japanese subway by the Aum Shinrikyo cult and also this cult was found to possess rudimentary biological weapons including anthrax botulism and Q fever. In 2001, anthrax powder was used as a biological weapon to kill people via mail system allegedly by Bin Laden terrorist group in USA. These incidents indicate that bioterrorism is on rise and it is a great threat to the civilized world.

Advantages and Disadvantages of Biological Warfare

Biological Warfare (BW) agents give advantages to the perpetrators. BW agents can cause large numbers of casualties with minimal logistical requirements. Perpetrators can escape long before BW agents cause casualties due to the incubation periods of agents. Weapons are easy and cheap to produce and can be used selectively target humans, animals or plants. The costs of conventional or nuclear weapons would far outstrip the bargain basement price of biological weapons to produce 50% casualties per square kilometre. BW agents can be easily procured from the environment, universities, biological supply houses and clinical specimens. Common fermentation techniques used for producing antibiotics, toxoid vaccines, foods, and beverages can be used to grow large quantities of BW agents. Simple aerosol generating devices mounted on planes or trucks can generate minute particles ideal for causing infectious aerosols. BW agents are invisible in aerosol clouds and not detectable until humans become ill. Panic would result as medical capabilities are quickly overwhelmed.

Counter Measures for Bioterrorism

Despite the International agreements to ban biological weapons under the 1925 Geneva protocol and the 1975 Biological and Toxin Weapons Convention, there is no effective international mechanism for challenging the development of biological weapons and their use. Advances in technology and the rise of fundamentalist terror groups present significant threat to world peace and democracy. A timely and definitive response to this threat will be proper cooperation between governments on a large scale and there is a need for proper planning, good communication between various departments and sufficient financial support for a realistic state of preparedness. Successfully meeting the challenges, of bioterrorism requires a multifaceted response. The key countermeasures for bioterrorism have been suggested by National Institute of Communicable Diseases. They include the following:

1. Prevention by reducing the opportunity with enhanced intelligence in collaboration with national and international agencies. All efforts should be made to reduce the aggression among groups and countries.
2. Deterrence by punishing the culprit without delay.
3. Strengthening epidemiological surveillance and capacity building. Surveillance should be developed for micro-organisms that can be used in bioterrorism.
4. Public health system need to be sensitized to capture the information and transmit to the appropriate authority if one gets any epidemiological clues of a biological warfare or terrorist attack.
5. Medical management by health promotion, specific protection by vaccination and personal measures, early diagnosis and treatment and disability limitation and rehabilitation.
6. All efforts should be made to formulate global strategies to handle religions and poverty to minimize or avoid biological war.

9

Science and Technology: Positive and Negative Impacts

Science is an attempt to discover order in nature and then use that knowledge to make predictions about what should happen in nature. Technology is the creation of products and processes intended to improve our efficiency, our chances for survival, our comfort level, and our quality of life. The goal of science is to develop widely accepted knowledge or ideas which are tangible; by contrast, technology is concerned primarily with the development of tangible things. Both science and technology blessed us with lots of amenities and comforts but these have cursed us in many ways. Our earliest ancestors were aware of the concept of technology and environment. They observed plants and animals, and learnt to protect themselves from harmful ones while made use of the others. They lived in a rich and competitive world closely to the environment. As hunters and gatherers, they knew a great deal about their surroundings. They knew the sources of water and use of plants and animals for food and medicine. The use of fire and various types of tools and weapons made their lives easier. Hunters and gatherers exploited the environment to fulfill their requirements. They cut down trees with axes and caused great changes in grasses and shrubs with the use of fire. However, they did not cause excessive damage to the environment due to their low population nomadic way of life and primitive technology. The domestication of plants and animals gave impetus to agricultural technology. With the increase in productivity of land crop production started increasing at a faster speed. Human populations started increasing beyond the limits previously fixed by natural food supply. The developments in machinery, fertilizers, pesticides and high yielding varieties caused unprecedented increase in agricultural productivity. The discovery of new medicine and improved sanitation enhanced human survival and population began a rapid ascent. Therefore, it is quite surprising to recall the speed of development from simple tools made from stones to the development of solid fuel propelled rockets. As modern man progressed with science and technology he turned to resources such as wood, coal, minerals and fossil fuels. In the process he learnt to master many forms of energy and matter, ultimately becoming manipulator of the environment with a power to change the destiny of the planet. The shifting role of man in the environment placed heavy demands on air, water and natural resources. As man gained control over the environment the link between him and nature weakened and he began to consider himself separate from and superior to nature. It is in this context that we must understand the use of science and technology and its negative impacts on the society and environment.

Agriculture and Biodiversity

Industrial revolution evolved into the green revolution which largely involves that extension of the same practices and methods that led to the advances in industry, biodiversity in agriculture has suffered. Large industrial sized farms have led to the proliferation of monocultures, whether for food (example, corn or wheat grown in hundreds or thousands of acres in the west or rice paddies in Asia or factory farms for cattle and poultry production bred for uniformity) or for timber (example managed forestry) in the tropics. These are susceptible to devastation by pests and biological organisms. Such large scale farming operations are efficient in terms of production since they are more conducive for automation. They do require ever increasing quantities of synthetic fertilizers, herbicides and pesticides and more vulnerable to viral, fungal, and bacterial diseases. The excessive use of fertilizers and pesticides contributes substantially to the ecological disturbances and environmental pollution. Excessive use of nitrogen fertilizers, for example can lead to leaching of these excessive fertilizers into the water bodies. These can be transformed by microorganisms into the nitrites and carcinogens such as nitrosamines and can find their way back to man and animals through the food chain. Excessive fertilizers can also adversely affect the nitrogen fixing organisms or microorganisms in the soil and reduce the natural nitrogen absorption and production of soils. Similarly, pesticides besides killing the unwanted pests, insects or birds can enter the human system through food or contact and become a health hazard. They can also indirectly come into the human system through animals which ingest the plants. The use of increased quantities of pumped or mined water results in falling water tables. There are serious concerns about the sustainability of such a large scale farming practices and the resilience of the monocultures in the presence of unknown and pesticide resistant organisms. The rush to modernize farming and the adoption of scientific methods are alienating farmers by slowly destroying local cultures. Knowledge of the local land, its unique characteristics including climate and the suitability of various plants are the resulting casualties.

Forests are the store houses of biodiversity. With growth in science and technology man has caused an onslaught on the forest cover in order to utilise forest resources for his needs and desires. Denudation of forest can cause long-term climatic changes by reducing rainfall and thus perpetuate and strengthen the desertification process over decades and sometimes over centuries. The courses of streams and rivers will also be affected. This denudation process destroys the ability of trees and the soil and humous which support shrubs, bushes, microorganisms, insects and animals which live in various symbiotic relationships with each other and the large plants or trees. Once the forest is gone, these animals, plants and other organisms are also destroyed making regeneration more difficult or impossible. When primitive man lived as a part of the ecological system he was one among the many species of animals which interacted with one another and with the physical world. Civilized man has gradually through the use of technology, transcended these symbiotic relationships to a considerable extent. This technology has given man a singular ability to interfere with or damage nature. If the ecological systems are destroyed or seriously disturbed, these have the potentiality of jeopardizing human welfare or if damage is great, of destroying human civilization.

Man's physical as well as mental health is connected to his symbiotic relationship with the ecological system in which he lives. A disease is considered to be a symptom of maladjustment with the ecological system. Man protected himself from disease in a variety of ways in historical times. The protection ways have become increasingly complex and sophisticated without increasing knowledge of nature. The concepts of our medical system have changed from that of treatment of diseases to their prevention. Prevention of disease is thought of as the maintenance of an equilibrium relationship of man with his environment and not as a creation of completely lifeless or sterile surroundings for human beings. It is neither desirable nor possible for human beings to live in a completely abiotic system; the concept of a relationship which enables man to remain healthy without forcing him to live in a sterile atmosphere has strong support in our current knowledge of the living world.

Urban and Rural Environment

Modern technology has caused drastic changes in the quality of our environment. The alterations in our environment have been speeded up the singular growth of human population. The expectations of people call for progressively greater availability of goods and services through processes of development. However, development requires utilization of our natural resources. The activities of man are compounded by factors of increasing technological ability, energy and material consumption and large population increase. The environmental impact of such increased activities is large and is increasingly global in character.

Man increasingly lives in large agglomerations in the urban settlements or small ones in rural areas. Human settlements are usually small and population densities low in rural agricultural fishing and forests areas. In these areas, large groups of people are counter productive because the land needed to support their needs of food, clothing and shelter increase beyond what the area can yield. The growth of modern technology and industry has increasingly helped to push up the population in urban settlements. In urban areas, the dynamics of population increase under the impact of modern technology have been to encourage large numbers of people to live close to industries and factories and to each other. The dynamics of industrialization and populations increase have led to the growth of the large modern urban complexes. The urban complexes show distinctive characters such as high density of population, high concentration of energy consumption and a high quantity of wastes and effluents that both industries and the large populations produce. The urban settlements are called urban ecosystems in which natural linkages have been largely destroyed or perverted and a new system of social and economic linkages have developed. As a result new sociological, psychological and technological problems have come into existence. The urban settlements are artificial in the sense that they are man-made and have different set of interactions and dynamics. The rural complexes on the other hand are closely related to their environment and the linkages within the natural ecosystem are not entirely disrupted because of low level technology use. The urban settlements are highly energy dependent while rural settlements depend on local energy resources. The urban settlements cause all environmental problems as artificial ecosystems while rural settlements being part of the natural ecosystems do not cause much pollution problems. This contrast is simply because of the use of various technologies by the urban settlements for the well-being as well as for having comforts.

Empowering Man for Various Tasks

The state of science and technology is that it empowered us to process what we need from nature more conveniently for more people, but the sense of awe and reverence that used to be present in our relationship to nature is often left behind. This is a primary reason that so many people now view the natural world is like a giant data bank that they can manipulate at will. The scientific and technological revolution has almost completely changed the physical realities of our relationship to the earth. Among all the problems arising out of the scientific revolution, the effect of nuclear weaponry on the perception of war has been singled out for special and intense scrutiny. Nuclear weapons pose an obvious and deadly threat and for the past fifty years, millions have protested that our world is unsafe as long as this technology is available for use during a war. It is extremely difficult to aggregate all the powerful new technologies affecting our relationship to the earth and the range of needs and desires we seek to satisfy with them. The cumulative impact of these technologies is qualitatively different from the cumulative impact of their predecessors but since there are so many of them, most performing services that have become integrated into our lives, it is very difficult to recognize this dramatic change in circumstances as historical event that has transformed our relationship to the earth. We have also fallen victims to a kind of technological hubris which tempts us to believe that our new powers may be unlimited. We dare to imagine that we will find technological solutions for every technologically induced problem. Our fascination with technology displaces what used to be a fascination with the wonder of nature. Like the young child who thinks bread originates on a store shelf we begin to forget that technology acts upon nature to meet our needs. As the population increases and our desire for higher rates of consumption continue to grow, we ask civilization for more of everything we want while ignoring the stress and strain tearing at the fabric of every natural system. We focus our attention more and more on using ecological processes to meet our needs, we numb the ability to feel our connections to the natural world. When we seek to artificially enhance our capacity to acquire what we need from the earth we do so at the direct expense of the earth's ability to provide naturally what we are seeking. When we increase agricultural production by using technologies that increase topsoil erosion we damage the land's ability to grow more food in the future. This agricultural technology further impacts the natural processes in a variety of ways. The shift from one technology to another even if the new one is used for the same basic purpose, can profoundly alter the relationship between different elements in a system. New generations of technology now appear so rapidly that the shift from one to the other can cause problems in our relationship to the environment. Sometimes, it is not the technology that changes but the setting in which it is used. A technology that was successful in the highland areas will not be successful in lowland areas with greater rainfall and different soil. In the same way, it is quite inappropriate to transplant the industrial culture that works well in a wealthy developed nation into a poor developing country where all the social conditions are different. Our relationship to technology can also be complicated by the way two or more powerful technologies interact with one another. We all are familiar with the occasional warnings on prescription medicine to alert us about potential drug interactions: two perfectly good medications, each useful and effective when taken alone in combination can cause an extremely harmful reaction. The same thing can occur with technologies. The scientific and technological revolution has picked up speed with great emphasis on technologies that extend and magnify abilities such as fighting wars. Our approach to technology itself has been shaped in such a way that devices take precedence over systems and ways to dominate nature receive more attention than ways to work with nature. The technological revolution has been disrupting the ecological balance of the world and apart from this, we have been intensifying more ways to manipulate nature.

Genetic engineering is a controversial but rapidly growing technology. Some see this biotechnology as a way to increase food supplies, degrade toxic wastes, eliminate certain genetic diseases and make enormous amounts of money. Some others fear that without strict controls, it could do great harm. Most recognize that it is unrealistic to stop genetic engineering altogether but they argue that it should be kept under strict control because we do not understand how nature works well enough to allow unregulated alteration of genetic characteristics of humans and other species. The most advanced form of biotechnology is cloning technology which has received worldwide criticism mostly on the basis of human ethics. Critics fear that unregulated biotechnology could lead to the development of super organisms. Bacteria genetically altered to clean up ocean oil spills by bio-chemically degrading the oil, would cause havoc if somehow they were able to multiply rapidly and began degrading the world's remaining oil supplies. Genetically engineered organisms might also mutate change, their form and behaviour, and then migrate. The widespread use of biotechnology is considered to pose serious effects and reduction in global biodiversity. Reducing the global biodiversity and hence the natural genetic diversity of wild plants and animals undermines genetic engineering ability to produce new genetic combinations. The controversial aspects of biotechnology illustrate the difficulty of balancing the actual and potential benefits of the technology with its actual and potential risks of harm.

Recent research in genetic engineering and biochemistry, eugenics and extra-uterine fertilization have brought to light the opportunity to manipulate life forms, something previously exclusively reserved to nature and chance. In this context, it can be said that morally irresponsible scientific development can release a monster that can destroy human civilization itself. The monster may declare that "remember that I have power....I can make you so wretched that the light of day will be hateful to you. You are my creator but I am your monster". Such a perception as seen in horror tales or movies can not be taken as a fantastic ghost story, but can be taken as a profound insight into the possible consequences of morally insensitive scientific and technological research.

Information Technology

Now-a-days we are witnessing the transformation from industrial to information society. This transformation has been considered by many that we are at the end of an era rather than the beginning of a new one. This technological revolution enabled us to have unparalleled knowledge and power over nature but at the same time, it crippled us with moral dilemmas and responsibilities for which we are ill-prepared. The humanity has not been able to find a proper solution to the moral dilemmas posed by the rapid technological change. Cyberspace or internet has really changed human life and in essence, it has become a part of life for many. It has been working as an addictive drug and people feel incomplete without it. Some people experience when they are unable to jack in for using internet. The internet has the potential to make us socially isolated, lonely and depressed. Spending time on the internet is associated with later declines in talking among family members, reduction in the number of friends and acquaintances they kept up with, and increases in depression and loneliness. Teenagers seem the most vulnerable to potential negative effects. It is no exaggeration to say that teenagers use the internet for more hours than adults do. Websites loaded with pornography have been spoiling the teenagers and youth who are the future guides of the social order. Cyberspace has in a way replaced the natural habitat of our species although it is something that does not exist as a real physical object. It is thought that the biodiversity and forest ecosystems will find place only in the world of cyberspace when life is created outside the natural order, self-destruction is inevitable. In a world where the sanctity of life and the miracle of birth no longer exist and where life can be interfaced and augmented with machines, life would no longer have value or meaning and death would lose its supposed sting. The obvious conclusion is that the human race always trying to go beyond its possibilities, has finally become prisoner not to its body but to something very inhuman in its kind and at the same time a product of its own intellect. Humanity has fallen victim to its greed for more, more at any price. In this aspiration for achievement, man has relentlessly continued to sever any links with nature. This civilized world, like an adolescent, acquired new powers but not the maturity to use the natural resources wisely. Therefore, the scientists who analyze, manipulate, and attempt to control nature unconsciously engage in a form of oppressive sex politics. Construing nature as the female partner, man attempts to make nature serve his own ends to gratify his own desires for power, wealth and reputation.

Role of Information Technology in Environment

Information Technology (IT), like previous revolutions such as electricity and the combustion engine, drives change in economies and societies around the world. IT also affects environmental issues, both in changing how goods are produced and consumed and also facilitating new means to address environmental challenges. The IT and Environment Initiative is an international consortium engaging in research and dissemination activities to improve understanding and awareness of the effects of the Information Technology revolution on environmental issues.

Areas of research being undertaken include:

- Environmental impacts and management of the production, use and disposal of IT equipment.
- Energy evaluations of IT business models and lifestyles changes such as e-commerce and telecommuting.
- Macro-economic analysis of the relationship between IT investments and energy use at the national level.
- Analysis of effects of IT-driven shifts in lifestyles and consumption pattern on embodied energy in consumption.

Acquisition, storage and processing of environmental information are becoming vital to preserving the quality of life. Potentially dangerous changes are happening in the atmosphere, oceans, animal habitats and places where hazardous materials are used, or have been discarded without adequate environmental protections. Terrorist attacks on buildings, water supplies and agricultural production and processing facilities, including the introduction of new, more virulent forms of animal diseases like anthrax, or spreading contamination in the form of nuclear waste could constitute potentially the most damaging environmental threat of our times.

In recent decades public interest in environmental problems has increased enormously, and research into these subjects has been intensifying. At the same time developments in computer and network techniques have led to the creation of sophisticated information systems with increased storage and transmission capacities. Such data can often be accessed by the public using the internet; and the public has become a very concerned participant in discussions about the environment.

In recent years, information technology has become significant to all scientific groups and fields involved in environment engineering. Knowledge based systems which enable the study of environmental changes have been developed, are being extended to manage those environments. New paradigms for designing objects to enable easy disassembly and recovery of components contribute to reuse. Developments in exploiting alternative energy sources are reducing dependence on non-renewable resources. Surveillance techniques enable tracking of persons likely to threaten the lives of persons or their environment.

Information Technology and Human Health

Health information technology (Health IT) allows comprehensive management of medical information and its secure exchange between health care consumers and providers. Broad use of health IT will:

- Improve health care quality;
- Prevent medical errors;
- Reduce health care costs;
- Increase administrative efficiencies;
- Decrease paperwork; and
- Expand access to affordable care.

Interoperable health IT will improve individual patient care, but it will also bring many public health benefits including:

- Early detection of infectious disease outbreaks around the country;

- Improved tracking of chronic disease management; and
- Evaluation of health care based on value enabled by the collection of de-identified price and quality information that can be compared.

Health information technologies can be tools that help individuals maintain their health through better management of their health information. Health IT will help consumers gather all of their health information in one place so they can thoroughly understand it and share it securely with their health care providers so they get the care that best fits their individual needs. Health IT can help to improve public health, one individual at a time by building partnerships between health care consumers and providers across the country.

10

ENVIRONMENTAL ECONOMICS AND SUSTAINABLE ARCHITECTURE

Environmental Economics

Environmental economics is a subfield of economics concerned with environmental issues. It is distinguished from green economics or ecological economics which includes the non-standard approaches to environmental problems, environmental science/environmental studies or ecology. It undertakes theoretical or empirical studies of the economic effects of national or local environmental policies around the world. Particular issues include the costs and benefits of alternative environmental policies to deal with air pollution, water quality, toxic substances, solid waste, and global warming.

Central to environmental economics is the concept of an externality. It means that some effects of an activity are not taken into account in its price. For instance, pollution in excess of the socially "optimal" level may occur if the prices a producer pays do not include the impacts (costs) experienced by those adversely affected. Visitors to an open-access recreational area will use the resource more than if they had to pay for it, leading to environmental degradation.

Environmental economics is based on ecosystem ecology. The focus is on energy at different trophic levels and its rate of flow among them, the distribution and flows of biochemical substances in soils and bodies of water, and of gases and particulates in the atmosphere. Economic studies of global warming, eutrophication of lakes, the management of range-lands, purification of water in watersheds, and the pollution estuaries are examples of such endeavour. Such studies provide valuable insights into the effects on ecosystems of the character of economic activities, as driven by technology, costs and revenues, discount rates, and the property-rights regime that govern the ecosystem.

Environmental Accounting

Environmental Accounting is a growing field that identifies resource use, measures and communicates costs of a company's or national ecomony actual or potential impact on the environment. Costs can include costs to clean up or remediate contaminated sites, environmental fines, penalties and taxes, purchase of pollution prevention technologies and waste management costs. An environmental accounting system is composed of environmentally differentiated conventional accounting and ecological accounting. Environmentally differentiated accounting measures impacts of the natural environment on a company in monetary terms while ecological accounting measures the impact a company has on the environment.

There are several reasons why businesses may consider adopting environmental accounting as part of their accounting system.

1. Possible significant reduction or elimination of environmental costs.
2. Environmental costs and benefits may be overlooked or hidden in overhead accounts.
3. Possible revenue generation may offset environmental costs.
4. Improved environmental performance which may have a positive impact on human health and business success.

5. May result in more accurate costing or pricing of products and more environmentally desired processes.
6. Possible competitive advantages as customers may prefer environmentally friendly products and services.
7. Can support the development and running of an overall environmental management system, which may be required by regulation for some types of businesses.

The accounting price of a resource is the increase in social well-being. It reflects social objectives, ecological and technological constraints, and the extent to which resources are available.

Costing Targets

The traditional cost approach "cost plus pricing" is inappropriate for today's liberalized environment. In traditional cost system, material, labour and overhead costs are measured and a desired profit is added to determine the selling price. Target Costing is defined as "a cost management tool for reducing the overall cost of a product over its entire life-cycle with the help of production, engineering, research and design". A target cost is the maximum amount of cost that can be incurred on a product and with it the firm can still earn the required profit margin from that product. It is that estimated cost which enables a firm to remain and compete in the market in the very long-run.

Target Costing is a simple, straightforward process that can have significant impact on the health and profitability of many, if not most, businesses. It does not require an army of specialists, large-scale software implementations or complex management structures and procedures. It is mostly logical, disciplined common sense that can be imbedded into a company's existing procedures and processes.

Target Costing helps to assure that products are better matched to their customer's needs, align the costs of features with customers' willingness to pay for them, reduce the development cycle of a product, reduce the costs of products significantly, increase the teamwork among all internal organizations associated with conceiving, marketing, planning, developing, manufacturing, selling, distributing and installing a product, and engage customers and suppliers to design the right product and to more effectively integrate the entire supply chain.

Sustainable procurement is a spending and investment process typically associated with public policy, although it is equally applicable to the private sector. Organizations practicing sustainable procurement meet their needs for goods, services, utilities and works not on a private cost-benefit analysis, but with a view to maximizing net benefits for themselves and the wider world. In doing so, they must incorporate exogenous considerations into decisions alongside the conventional procurement criteria of price and quality. These considerations are typically divided thus, environmental, economic and social also known as the "triple baseline".

Environmental concerns are the dominant macro-level justification for sustainable procurement; born out of the growing 21st century consensus that humanity is placing excessive demands on available resources through unsustainable but well-established consumption patterns. This is a sufficiently influential issue that environment-centric procurement is sometimes seen to stand alone from sustainable procurement. The most straightforward justification for green procurement is a tool with which to address climate change, but it offers the broader capacity to mitigate over-exploitation of any and all scarce resources.

Green procurement means the procurement of products and services that have less impact on the environment than their traditional counterparts. Greener procurement incorporates environmental considerations into decisions in addition to the conventional criteria of price and quality. In support of sustainable development, the organization should develop and publish a "Sustainable Development Procurement Guidelines and Procedures". When it comes to purchasing products or services, referral to these guidelines would help make the organization become a leader in environmentally responsible purchasing.

Sustainable design also referred to as "green design" or "eco-design" or "design for environment" is the art of designing physical objects to comply with the principles of economic, social and ecological sustainability. The essential aim of sustainable design is to produce products and services in a way that reduces use of non-renewable resources, minimizes environmental impact, and relates people with the natural environment. Sustainable design is often viewed as a necessary tool for achieving sustainability. It is related to the more heavy-industry-focused fields of industrial ecology and green chemistry, sharing tools such as lifecycle assessment and lifecycle energy analysis to judge the environmental impact or "greenness" of various design choices. It ranges from the microcosm of designing small objects for everyday use, through to the macrocosm of designing buildings, cities, and the earth's physical surface. It is a growing trend within the fields of architecture, landscape architecture, engineering, graphic design, industrial design, interior design and fashion design.

Sustainable design is a reaction to the global "environmental crisis", i.e., rapid growth of economic activity and human population, depletion of natural resources, damage to ecosystems and loss of biodiversity. Proponents of sustainable design believe that the crisis is in large part caused by conventional design and industrial practices, which disregard the risks and environmental impacts associated with goods and services. Green design is considered a means of reducing or eliminating these impacts while maintaining quality of life by using careful assessment and clever design to substitute less harmful products and processes for conventional ones.

Principles of sustainable design include

- Low-impact materials: choose non-toxic, sustainably-produced or recycled materials which require little energy to process.
- Energy efficiency: use manufacturing processes and produce products which require less energy.
- Quality and durability: longer-lasting and better-functioning products will have to be replaced less frequently, reducing the impacts of producing replacements.
- Design for reuse and recycling: products, processes and systems should be designed for performance in a commercial 'afterlife'.
- Biomimicry: redesigning industrial systems on biological lines enabling the constant reuse of materials in continuous closed cycles.
- Service substitution: shifting the mode of consumption from personal ownership of products to provision of services which provide similar functions.
- Renewability: materials should come from nearby local or bioregional, sustainably-managed renewable sources that can be composted or fed to livestock when their usefulness has been exhausted.

Sustainable Architecture

It is the design of sustainable buildings. Sustainable architecture attempts to reduce the collective environmental impacts during the production of building components, during the construction process, as well as during the lifecycle of the building. This design practice emphasises efficiency of heating and cooling systems, alternative energy sources such as passive solar, appropriate building siting, reused or recycled building materials, *on-site* power generation, rain water harvesting for gardening and washing, and on-site waste management such as green roots that filter and control storm water runoff. Sustainable architects design with sustainable living in mind.

Sustainable Landscape Architecture

It is a category of sustainable design concerned with the planning and design of outdoor space. This can include ecological, social and economic aspects of sustainability. Design techniques include planting trees to shade buildings from the sun or protect them from wind, using local materials, on-site composting and chipping to reduce greenwaste hauling, and also may involve using drought-resistant plantings in arid areas and buying stock from local growers to avoid energy use in transportation.

Sustainable Technologies

Sustainable technologies use less energy, fewer limited resources, do not deplete natural resources, do not directly or indirectly pollute the environment, and can be reused or recycled at the end of their useful life. There is a significant overlap with appropriate technology, which emphasizes the suitability of technology to the context, in particular considering the needs of people in developing countries. However, the most appropriate technology may not be the most sustainable one; and a sustainable technology may have high cost or maintenance requirements that make it unsuitable as an "appropriate technology".

Environmental Design

Environmental design in the old-fashioned sense develops physical environments, both interior and exterior, to meet one or more aesthetic or day-to-day functional needs, or to create a specific sort of experience - the focus being the human-designed environment. It includes specialities such as architects, acoustical scientists, engineers, environmental scientists, landscape architects, urban planning, interior designers, lighting designers, and exhibition designers. In many situations, historic preservation can be added to this list.

Zero-energy Building

It is a general term applied to a building with a net energy consumption of zero over a typical year. This can be measured in different ways relating to cost, energy, or carbon emissions and, irrespective of the definition used, different views are taken on the relative importance of energy generation and energy conservation to achieve energy balance. Although zero energy buildings remain uncommon in developed countries, they are gaining importance and popularity. The zero-energy approach is promoted as a potential solution to a range of social and environmental issues, including reducing carbon emissions, reducing dependence on oil power, fuel imports, and the use of fossil fuels in general, and providing a measure of energy security against future energy crises. Most definitions do not include the emissions generated in the construction of the building and the embodied energy of the structure which would usually invalidate claims of reducing carbon emissions.

To achieve minimal energy use, the design and construction of zero energy buildings depart significantly from conventional building practice. In conventional building design the emphasis is normally on minimizing construction costs. Designers rarely do any energy analysis or lifecycle operating cost calculations beyond those necessary to comply with local building codes. In the ZEB approach, every decision about major sub-system selection is evaluated in terms of its future consequences on energy demand using lifecycle energy analysis. ZEB designers are usually prepared to increase construction costs if doing so will reduce energy demand and operating costs by an equal or greater amount. The ZEB approach might be described as "energy first" building design. In addition to using renewable sources, zero energy buildings are also designed to make use of energy gained from other sources including white goods, lighting, and even body heat. Furthermore, these buildings make use of heat energy that conventional buildings typically let go to waste by use of heat recovery ventilation and hot water heat recycling units. They are normally optimised to use passive solar heat gain, use thermal mass to even out temperature variations throughout the day, and in most climates are super-insulated. All the technologies needed to create zero energy buildings are available off the shelf today.

Energy Generation

In the case of individual houses, various microgeneration technologies may be used to provide heat and electricity to the building, perhaps using solar cells or wind turbines for electricity, and biofuels, or solar collectors linked to seasonal thermal stores, for space heating. To cope with fluctuations in demand, zero energy buildings are frequently connected to the electricity grid, and may export electricity to it when there is a surplus.

Energy Conservation

It is the practice of decreasing the quantity of energy used while achieving a similar outcome. This practice may result in increase of financial capital, environmental value, national security, personal security, and human comfort. Individuals and organizations that are direct consumers of energy may want to conserve energy in order to reduce energy costs and promote economic, political and environmental sustainability. Industrial and commercial users may want to increase efficiency and thus maximize profit. On a larger scale, energy conservation is an important element of energy policy. In general, energy conservation reduces the energy consumption and energy demand per capita, and thus offsets the growth in energy supply needed to keep up with population growth. This reduces the rise in energy costs, and can reduce the need for new power plants, and energy imports. The reduced energy demand can provide more flexibility in choosing the most preferred methods of energy production. By reducing emissions, energy conservation is an important part of lessening climate change. Energy conservation facilitates the replacement of non-renewable resources with renewable energy. Energy conservation is often the most economical solution to energy shortages, and is a more environmentally benign alternative to increased energy production.

Green Building

Green building is the practice of increasing the efficiency of buildings and their use of, and reducing building impacts on human health and the environment, through better siting, design, construction, operation, maintenance, and removal – the complete building lifecycle. The related concepts of sustainable development and sustainability are integral to green building. Green building often emphasizes taking advantage of renewable resources, such as using sunlight through passive solar, active solar, and photovoltaic techniques and using plants and trees through green roofs, rain gardens, and for reduction of rainwater run-off. Many other techniques, such as using packed gravel for parking lots instead of concrete or asphalt to enhance replenishment of groundwater, are used as well. Effective green building can lead to 1) reduced operating costs by increasing productivity and using less energy and water, 2) improved public and occupant health due to improved indoor air quality, and 3) reduced environmental impacts. Practitioners of green building often seek to achieve not only ecological but aesthetic harmony between a structure and its surrounding natural and built environment. The sustainable buildings are also environmental friendly in the fact that they are built out of materials that are good for the environment. The appearance and style of sustainable homes and buildings can be nearly indistinguishable from their less sustainable counterparts.

Green building brings together a vast array of practices and techniques to reduce and ultimately eliminate the impacts of buildings on the environment. On the aesthetic side of green architecture or sustainable design is the philosophy of designing a building that is in harmony with the natural features and resources surrounding the site. There are several key steps in designing sustainable buildings: specify 'green' building materials from local sources, reduce loads, optimize systems, and generate on-site renewable energy. Building materials typically considered to be 'green' include rapidly renewable plant materials like bamboo and straw, lumber from forests certified to be sustainably managed, stone, recycled metal, and other products that are non-toxic, reusable, renewable, and/or recyclable. Building materials should be extracted and manufactured locally to the building site to minimize the energy embedded in their transportation. Low-impact building materials are used wherever feasible. To minimize the energy loads within and on the structure, it is critical to orient the building to take advantage of cooling breezes and sunlight. Daylighting with ample windows will eliminate the need to turn on electric lights during the day. Passive Solar can warm a building in the winter but care needs to be taken to provide shade in the summer time to prevent overheating. Prevailing breezes and convection currents can passively cool the building in the summer. Thermal mass stores heat gained during the day and releases it at night minimizing the swings in temperature. Thermal mass can both heat the building in winter and cool it during the summer. Insulation is the final step to optimizing the structure. Well-insulated windows, doors, and walls help reduce energy loss, thereby reducing energy usage. These design features do not cost much money to construct and significantly reduce the energy needed to make the building comfortable. Optimizing the heating and cooling systems through installing energy efficient machinery, commissioning, and heat recovery is the next step. Compared to optimizing the passive heating and cooling features through design, the gains made by engineering are relatively expensive and can add significantly to the projects cost. However, thoughtful integrated design can reduce costs.

Natural Building

The building is usually on a smaller scale and tends to focus on the use of natural materials that are available locally. It involves a range of building systems and materials that place major emphasis on sustainability. Ways of achieving sustainability through natural building focus on durability and the use of minimally-processed, plentiful or renewable resources, as well as those which, while recycled or salvaged, produce healthy living environments and maintain indoor air quality. Natural building tends to rely on human labor, more than technology. The basis of natural building is the need to lessen the environmental impact of buildings and other supporting systems, without sacrificing comfort, health or aesthetics. To be more sustainable, natural building uses primarily abundantly-available, renewable, reused or recycled materials. The use of rapidly renewable materials is increasingly a focus. An emphasis on building compactly and minimizing the ecological footprint is common, as are on-site handling of energy acquisition, on-site water capture, alternate sewage treatment and water reuse. Other green building strategies that improve conservation of resources include: rain-water catchment, storage, and purification; waste-water separation; biological waste-water purification and grey-water reuse; composting toilets, on-site snow/rain-water run-off management; permeable paving; native or low-water-use ("xeriscape") landscapes, and accommodation of alternative-fuelled/powered and human-powered vehicles.

Green Roof

A green roof is roof of a building that is partially or completely covered with vegetation and soil, or a growing medium, planted over a waterproofing membrane. This does not refer to roofs which are merely colored green. It may also include additional layers such as a root barrier and drainage and irrigation systems. Container gardens on roofs, where plants are maintained in pots, are not generally considered to be true green roofs. The term "green roof" may also be used to indicate roofs that utilize some form of "green" technology, such as solar panels or a photovoltaic module. Green roofs are also referred to as eco-roofs, vegetated roofs, living roofs, and green roofs. Green roofs are used to provide amenity space for building users, grow fruits, vegetables, and flowers, reduce heating and cooling loads on a building, reduce the urban heat island effect, increase roof life span, reduce stormwater run off, filter pollutants and carbon dioxide out of the air, filter pollutants and heavy metals out of rainwater, and increase wildlife habitat in built-up areas.

Green Transport

It is a category of sustainable transport which uses human power, animal power and renewable energy. In common usage, public transport is considered a green transport option in comparison with private vehicles, as is car pooling. But some people prefer a definition that does not include public transport or vehicle movements which relies on non-renewable energy. Green transport includes walking, cycling and some other types of human-powered transport, solar powered vehicles, and wind powered vehicles. Often, there can be a sliding scale of green transport depending on the sustainabilty of the option. Public transport on traditional diesel buses uses less fuel per passenger than private vehicles so is more green than private vehicles, but is not as green as using a solar powered bus.

Ecocity

The idea of Eco cities, sustainable city or Ecopolis is a new approach toward sustainable living. Environmentalists used to believe that city living was pollutive and destructive to the environment because of the huge amount of sewage, trash, and unsanitary conditions created and dumped into the environment. An ecocity means working together for a better social, economic, and environmental outcomes for our children, our grandchildren, and ourselves. It means working with people and communities to build a strong local economy, create attractive town-centers with good roads and passenger transport access, protect and expand the "green network", use resources better, and produce less waste, and improving the well-being of residents.

Ecovillages

Ecovillages are intended to be socially, economically and ecologically sustainable intentional communities. Ecovillage members are united by shared ecological, social or spiritual values. An ecovillage is often composed of people who have chosen an alternative to centralized power, water and sewage systems. Many see the breakdown of traditional forms of community, wasteful consumerist lifestyles, the destruction of natural habitat, urban sprawl, factory farming, and over-reliance on fossil fuels, as trends that must be changed to avert ecological disaster. They see small-scale communities with minimal ecological impact as an alternative. However, such communities often cooperate with peer villages in networks of their own.

The principles on which ecovillages rely can be applied to urban and rural settings, as well as to developing and developed countries. Advocates seek infrastructural independence and a sustainable lifestyle for inhabitants with a minimum of trade outside the local area, or ecoregion. Rural ecovillages are usually based on organic farming, permaculture and other approaches which promote ecosystem function and biodiversity. Some ecovillages integrate many of the design principles of cohousing, but with a greater ecological focus and a more "organic" process, typical of permaculture design. An ecovillage usually relies on "green" infrastructural capital, autonomous building or clustered housing, to minimize ecological footprint, renewable energy, permaculture, cohousing or other forms of supportive community. Its organization also usually depends upon some instructional capital or moral codes. Local purchasing so as to support the local economy, local food production and distribution, consensus decision-making for governance, and a choice to respect diversity.

Xeriscaping

Xeriscaping refers to landscaping in ways that do not require supplemental irrigation. It is promoted in areas that do not have easily accessible supplies of fresh water. The word Xeriscaping was coined by combining xeros with landscape. Plants whose natural requirements are appropriate to the local climate are emphasized, and care is taken to avoid losing water to evaporation and run-off. Some common plants used in xeriscaping are agave, cactus, lavender, juniper, sedum and thyme.

Implementation of xeriscaping includes appropriate choice and arrangement of a plant (s), where possible, plants that are native to the area or to similar climates, as well as other plants that tolerate or avoid water stress (xerophytes, halophytes, summer-dormant bulbs, and very deeply rooted plants) as ornamentals. Hydrozoning, grouping plants with similar watering requirements together is quite necessary. Plants that require more water (for example, vegetables, fruits, and certain flowers) are grouped together. These plants may also be sheltered from the wind and/or sun by planting them in the shade to decrease the amount of water they need. The landscape can be filled in with borders and islands of more water-efficient ornamental plants. Efficient application of water is done by using drip irrigation where possible. Overhead irrigation is applied in the morning or evening, when it is less likely to be blown away by wind or lost by evaporation. Drought-tolerant plants get no more water than they need to look good. Soil with improved structure retains water better, and mulch cools the soil surface and hinders evaporation. Advantages of xeriscaping include lower water bills, more water available for other uses and other people such as showers, sinks, hoses, less time and work needed for maintenance, making gardening more simple and stress-free.

Worldviews

"The world" is the broadest environment that is cognitively, practically and emotionally relevant. "The world" should not be identified with "the earth," nor with "the cosmos," nor with "the observable universe," but with the totality in which we live and to which we can relate ourselves in a meaningful way.

A world view is a coherent collection of concepts and theorems that must allow us to construct a global image of the world, and in this way to understand as many elements of our experience as possible. Societies, as well as individuals, have always contemplated deep questions relating to their being and becoming, and to the being and becoming of the world. The configuration of answers to these questions forms their world view. A world view is a system of co-ordinates or a frame of reference in which everything presented to us by our diverse experiences can be placed. It is a symbolic system of representation that allows us to integrate everything we know about the world and ourselves into a global picture, one that illuminates reality as it is presented to us within a certain culture.

World-view construction consists of the attempt to develop world views that take into account as much as possible all aspects of our experience. It is always connected to a culture in which "meanings" are circulated, types of behaviour are passed from generation to generation, socio-political problems are produced, and styles of art confront us. The material used to construct a world view comes from our inner experience and our practical dealings with things, as well as from the interpretation of history and of scientific knowledge about our world. All these aspects are necessarily related to particular cultures, which are not monolithic entities, but which are always in a process of change. In this sense world views are not fixed images or copies of the world, but will somehow try to capture, as much as is possible, all the aspects of this world. Therefore new world views often start with the views of small groups or sub-cultures, and prepare, step by step, new concepts of reality. They are not just a reflection of "what everybody thinks." World view construction, as we see it, consciously aims at collective work that is not identifiable with one person. It groups specialists of divergent disciplines, and aspires to ultimately express itself in forms that can reach a large public. In this sense, world view construction inevitably has a collective dimension. The human and social sciences continuously provide us with a deeper insight into the nature of man and society. A world view cannot contradict known experimental facts, but this does not mean that it coincides with them. A world view may even inspire further development of science and if necessary, from a synthetic vantage point, criticize certain one-sided aspects of it. In this sense, a world view is a continuation of what the sciences pass on to us, sometimes coinciding with it, sometimes generalizing from it, and sometimes critically rejecting it.

Everyone who wants to construct a reasonable view of reality and human existence will have to take into account the following questions:

1. What is happiness and suffering for feeling and/or conscious beings?
2. What increases or decreases happiness and suffering?
3. What is the meaning and the function of aesthetic experience? What is beauty and ugliness? How can these categories be applied to the physical, biological, social and psychological world? Can they be applied to the world as a whole?
4. What is the origin of the distinction between good and evil? Can these concepts be applied to different regions of reality, or are they limited to the human world? What determines the values that someone will choose in his or her personal life? What is the meaning of the distinction between the healthy and the sick, between the normal and the abnormal? Is this distinction only culturally determined?

According to conventional wisdom, He produced a lousy world, filled with miserable people - which is why we must reverse his work and must change the world, transforming it as radically as possible. This transformation is to be achieved by means of science, technology, industry and the various institutions of the nation-state, which together will supposedly bring about that miraculous process called 'economic development', or 'progress', thus creating a veritable paradise on earth; one that is incomparably superior to any that God or even the evolutionary process could possibly bring about. This is unquestionably the most pernicious myth ever entertained by man; the policies followed are leading to inexorable destruction of the biosphere, which in turn inevitably spells the eventual extinction of our species. The economic development involves methodically substituting the technosphere or the surrogate world of human artifacts for the biosphere or the real world of living things from which the former derives its resources and to which it consigns its ever more voluminous and toxic waste products. In other words, economic development, to which our society is totally committed, inevitably means ecological degradation and economic contraction. The two are inseparable but different sides of the same coin. Ecological degradation and contraction gives rise to a host of problems, each one of which is interpreted in such a way as to make it appear amenable to a solution that involves further economic development. Such an interpretation is consistent with the world view of modernism. Thus, we are told, the population explosion is caused by poverty and insecurity in the 'underdeveloped' countries, and the only way to solve it is through further economic development which will make the poor, rich and secure and thereby give rise to the so-called 'demographic transition', with birth rates falling as material prosperity increases. We are in effect caught up in a veritable chain reaction in the direction of ever greater biospheric destruction and eventual human extinction. Indeed, if man is to survive on this planet for more than a few decades, then our society must not only be restructured into socio-economic groupings that are capable of sustaining themselves without annihilating the world of living things, but we must also reject the world view of modernism in all its ramification, replacing it with a world view that validates these very different socio-economic structures and their ecologically benign policies.

The 'technospheric' world view of modernism needs to be replaced with a new 'ecological' world view, but to achieve this, green thinkers must concentrate on the great principles that unite them, not on the doctrines that divide them. The progressive degradation of the biosphere which we are witnessing today cannot be attributed to technical deficiencies in the implementation of our socio-economic policies. It is the policies themselves that by their very nature are causing the destruction. We have all become dependent on the proper functioning of commercial, bureaucratic and political institutions which employ the bulk of us, and which are committed to and dependent on the perpetuation of precisely those policies that are causing the destruction. The world view of modernism rationalizes and legitimizes these policies and brings about the destruction of the environment.

The biocentric view, forwarded by the deep ecology movement holds that all species have intrinsic value and that humans are no more important than other species. Thus everything has an equal right to exist simply because it already exists. Having this right will result in also having a "right" to have ones future survival guaranteed to an extent equal to any and all other species. If one accepts the idea that biodiversity has intrinsic value, then species conservation requires less justification. In other words, if a species is intrinsically valuable, regardless of its use to humans or to other species, it should be conserved, and then the onus is on those who do not want to conserve the species to provide a justification for its removal. Intrinsic value is a central tenet of many religions. Many religions consider everything on earth to be inherently sacred, or sacred as a result of being created by a divine being, and thus, intrinsically valuable, and humans are responsible to care for and respect these creations.

Bibliography

Alexander, D.E. (1999). Encyclopedia of Environmental Science, Springer.

Anil Kumar, De, (1995). Environmental Chemistry, Third Edition, Wiley Eastern Limited. New Age International Limited.

Chichilnisky, G. and Heal, G.M. (1998). Economic returns from the biosphere. Nature 391: 629.

Costanza, R.R. (ed.) (1991). Ecological Economics: The Science and Management of Sustainability. Columbia University Press, New York.

Malhotra, Y. (1993). Role of Information Technology in Managing Organizational Change and Organizational Interdependence. www. brint.com.

Nordhaus, W.D. (1994). Managing the Global Commons: The Economics of Climate Change. MIT Press, Cambridge, MA.

Perrings, C. and Walker, B.W. (1995). Biodiversity loss and the economics of discontinuous change in semi-arid rangelands. In: C. Perrings, et al. (eds.), Biodiversity Loss: Economic and Ecological Issues. Cambridge University Press, Cambridge.

Perrings, C., Maler, K.G., Folke, C., Holling, C.S. and Jansson, B.O. (eds.) (1994). Biodiversity Conservation: Problems and Policies. Klewer, Dordrecht.

Perrings, C., Maler, K.G., Folke, C., Holling, C.S. and Jansson, B.O. (eds.) (1995). Biodiversity Loss: Economic and Ecological Issues. Cambridge University Press, Cambridge.

Sustainability analysis for irrigation water management: concepts, methodology, and application to the Aral Sea region. Ximing Cai, Daene C. McKinney, and Mark W.R. Environment and Production Technology Division, International Food Policy Research Institute, Washington, D.C.

The Water (Prevention and Control of Pollution) Cess Act, 1977. Ministry of Law, Justice and Company Affairs (Legislative Department), New Delhi.

http://en.wikipedia.org/wiki/Acid_rain

http://en.wikipedia.org/wiki/Air_pollution

http://en.wikipedia.org/wiki/Atmosphere

http://en.wikipedia.org/wiki/Biodiversity

http://en.wikipedia.org/wiki/Bioremediation

http://en.wikipedia.org/wiki/Climate_change

http://en.wikipedia.org/wiki/Conservation_biology

http://en.wikipedia.org/wiki/Dam

http://en.wikipedia.org/wiki/Drought

http://en.wikipedia.org/wiki/Earth's_atmosphere

http://en.wikipedia.org/wiki/Ecosystem

http://en.wikipedia.org/wiki/Environmentalism

http://en.wikipedia.org/wiki/Flood

http://en.wikipedia.org/wiki/Global_warming

http://en.wikipedia.org/wiki/Species_diversity

http://en.wikipedia.org/wiki/Sustainable_development

http://en.wikipedia.org/wiki/Sustainable_energy

http://en.wikipedia.org/wiki/Waste_minimisation

http://en.wikipedia.org/wiki/Wastewater

http://en.wikipedia.org/wiki/Water_Cycle

http://en.wikipedia.org/wiki/Water_pollution

http://en.wikipedia.org/wiki/Water_quality

http://en.wikipedia.org/wiki/Water_resources

http://en.wikipedia.org/wiki/Waterborne_diseases

http://en.wikipedia.org/wiki/Watershed

http://en.wikipedia.org/wiki/Watershed_management

http://www.forestresources.com/

http://www.forestresources.org/

INDEX